e Poconos

Ghosts of the

L'Aura
Hladik Hoffman

Schiffer
Publishing Ltd

4880 Lower Valley Road • Atglen, PA 19310

Poconos

Designed by RoS
Cover design by Justin Watkinson

Type set in Bleeding Cowboys/Amerigo BT

ISBN: 978-0-7643-5251-5
Printed in China

Published by Schiffer Publishing, Ltd.
4880 Lower Valley Road
Atglen, Pennsylvania 19310
Phone: (610) 593-1777; Fax: (610) 593-2002
E-mail: Info@schifferbooks.com
Web: www.schifferbooks.com

For our complete selection of fine books on this and related subjects, please visit our website at www.schifferbooks.com. You may also write for a free catalog.

Schiffer Publishing's titles are available at special discounts for bulk purchases for sales promotions or premiums. Special editions, including personalized covers, corporate imprints, and excerpts, can be created in large quantities for special needs. For more information, contact the publisher.

We are always looking for people to write books on new and related subjects. If you have an idea for a book, please contact us at proposals@schifferbooks.com.

This book is dedicated to my Dad.

He made sure I saw the televised history-making landing
on the moon in 1969 and introduced me to the classic
Twilight Zone television series. His love, guidance,
and sense of humor are timeless
and boundless gifts to me.

Contents

Acknowledgments

I extend my special thanks and appreciation to ALL who helped me and contributed to this book. The time you spent telling me about your ghostly encounters and experiences was riveting and valuable to the credibility of the material included in this work.

I would also like to thank John Hotchkiss for his help with The Shawnee Inn, Sorrenti's Winery, and Pocono Cinema chapters. To fellow authors Charles J. Adams III, Rosemary Ellen Guiley, and Kenneth Biddle, thank you! Your tireless work and research were invaluable to me in this project.

Thank you to Melissa D'Agastino, Team Leader for the Central Jersey Division of the New Jersey Ghost Hunters Society. You are a dedicated paranormal investigator. I am so glad you were with me when we were alone investigating the dungeon of the Old Jail in Jim Thorpe. I'm not sure if I ever showed you the video I captured that day. It shows a bug, the size of my fist, crawling across the dungeon floor. Ghosts, residual haunts . . . tolerable . . . creepy crawlies, well, not so much.

Of course, thanks to my husband, Kent. You're quite an accomplished ghost hunter now and even better at turning a blind eye to the dishes piled in the sink while I was feverishly writing this book. I know you think the computer will have to be surgically removed from my fingers, but rest assured that is not the case. Your love, support, and patience during this stressful, monumental, and fascinating project mean so much to me. Again, thank you.

Introduction

"Welcome to Pennsylvania. America starts here." Growing up in Jersey, I always found this sign that was conspicuously posted as one crossed the Delaware Water Gap from New Jersey into Pennsylvania, particularly offensive. I took it to mean this vast, expansive state (Pennsylvania) was "dissing" my little New Jersey.

That is definitely not the case. Having lived in the Poconos for the past four years, I can attest to the warm and welcoming character of the people who live here. Most of these people have been here for generations. There are several notable family lines such as the Strouds, the Saylors, and the Werkheissers.

Then there is the history, which traces back 8,000 years with the original inhabitants being that of the Lenni-Lenape Native American tribe. From the growing pains of Dutch and Germans settling in the area, to the American Revolutionary War through the Civil War and up to current times, the Poconos has seen all the facets of America's history evolve.

The namesake of the state is William Penn. He was born in London in 1644, and at the age of thirty-seven he came to the New World and was granted sovereignty over the 45,000 square miles of land King Charles II gave him as a debt repayment owed to William Sr. Naming this land was a combination of "Sylvania," Latin for woods or forest and William's surname as homage to his father, a former admiral in the British Navy.

Penn established Philadelphia, from the Greek meaning "city of brotherly love," at the base of the Delaware River. Waterways are keys to establishing viable communities as they provide transportation of goods, as well as access to life-sustaining water for drinking and watering of crops. By 1682, Lord Baltimore from Maryland was claiming that the area of Philadelphia belonged to him via his charter from the King. Penn dismissed this claim, and it was not until the establishment of the Mason-Dixon Line, 1763, that these lands and their respective ownership were definitively determined.

Having converted to Quakerism at the age of twenty-two, Penn governed his territory with an overriding sense of fairness to all concerned: Native Americans, Dutch, German, and British. He set up his government as an assembly comprised of two legislative houses to protect citizens' property and businesses and to impose taxes equitably. In 1701, the Charter of Privileges was completed by Penn. This document was in force until the

beginning of the American Revolution. Subsequently, it was replaced by the State Constitution.

In 1718, nineteen years after William Penn's death, his son, Thomas Penn, and James Logan wanted to purchase land situated north of the established borderline to accommodate the steady population growth and continued influx of European settlers. The natives were not receptive to this desired expansion, and, therefore, Logan devised a plan to survey the land targeted. This plan became known as the "Walking Purchase." Basically beginning in Wrightstown, the tract of land would extend northward as far as a man could walk in a day and a half.

Apparently, the colonists' definition of "walk" was not the same as that of the Delaware Indians. One could view this as cheating since the Penn team members were moving at a running pace, certainly not a walking pace. Of the three men hired to represent Penn's team, only one, Edward Marshall, lasted the day and a half and completed sixty-five miles ending at present day Jim Thorpe, Pennsylvania. He was compensated with 500 acres of land, which today is known as Marshalls Creek.

The Iroquois were brought in to help remove the Delaware Natives from this newly, somewhat underhandedly acquired, 1,200 square miles of land. The Delaware Natives never forgave Marshall and attacked his family on two separate occasions. In the first attack of 1747, Marshall's son was killed, and in the second attack of 1756, his wife was killed and scalped.

In the late 1800s, the Poconos morphed into a seasonal vacation location with the Buckwood Inn and other resorts that followed. Today, the resorts operate year-round. Even the water parks have been enclosed to accommodate family fun in any season, and in any weather. There is plenty here to please the "outdoorsy" types with skiing, hiking, ice skating, bicycling, canoeing, fishing, and white water rafting. For those who prefer to remain indoors, there are the spas of Shawnee and the Laurel Spa at Pocono Manor. The restaurant selection ranges from pub grub to fine dining. The Mount Airy Casino provides the gambling excitement of Atlantic City with the mountain vistas of the Poconos.

For the ghost hunter, well, it is a paranormal playground as well. Use this book as a travel guide to the haunted locations. Please respect "no trespassing" signs when posted. And, please, do not use this book as your "express pass" to impose on business owners and wait staff. If your server or bartender is kind enough to spend a little extra time talking about the haunted activity of their establishment, please tip generously.

CHAPTER 1

The Tannersville Inn

Hot Buffalo wings and cold spots. Meet the ghost of Mable.

The legendary, as it is affectionately referred to by its owners and locals, Tannersville Inn is in the heart of Tannersville on Route 611. Its construction dates back to 1825 and it is, therefore, the oldest operating restaurant in the Poconos. The original front of the building faced the main street that provided for commerce and people to travel between Scranton and Easton, Pennsylvania. To put the age of the Tannersville Inn into perspective, John Quincy Adams was president of the United States when the doors officially opened for business. In 1847, Manasseh Miller purchased the building and its ninety-eight acres and dubbed his new venture The Tannersville Hotel. His picture, taken on the original front porch of the hotel in 1850, is visible on the fireplace mantle in the main dining room.

In January 2015, I interviewed the manager of the restaurant, Bob Jakubowitz. His family bought the Tannersville Inn in 1972. They set out to make the inn a comfortable place to dine and unwind. It's perfectly located for those day-trippers who shop the outlets at the Crossings and for those vacationers who ski at Camelback. The menu includes "pub grub" of chicken wings and loaded french fries to higher-end dining of surf & turf. Honestly, the wafts of chicken wings in the tavern made it very challenging for me to focus on the interview.

There are several dining areas that comprise the Tannersville Inn: the tavern, the main dining room, the green house, parlor, and veranda. Bob and I started our conversation in the main dining room. Around 2004, Bob had his first otherworldly experience as the restaurant's manager. It was late, approximately 2:40 a.m., when he was finishing up paperwork and one of the waitresses was chatting with him. His paperwork is filed in a beautiful antique dresser. While he was rummaging through the drawers of the dresser and sorting papers, he looked up to respond to the waitress, and at that moment he saw a shadow glide across the wall above the dresser. This shadow was very pronounced given the forty-watt light bulb in the sconce on the wall he had his back towards. He turned around very quickly to see who had passed by behind him to cast the shadow, but no one was there. He looked at the waitress who had a very perplexed expression on her face. She did not see the shadow go by on the wall above the dresser and, therefore, didn't understand why Bob had spun around so abruptly to face the wall behind him. He asked her: "Did you see that?" She replied: "See what?"

The height at which the shadow appeared on the wall indicates someone—or something—being tall in stature. A living person casting this shadow certainly would not have gone

Orb in front parlor.

unnoticed by the waitress who was facing in that general direction while talking with Bob.

Bob continued my tour by taking me to the original front of the building to see the parlor. For approximately fifteen years, the restaurant hosted Murder Mystery Dinners in this room. Currently, it is used primarily for private dinner parties and small gatherings, such as bridal showers and wedding rehearsal dinners. It was in this room that I captured an orb hovering by the one corner of the fireplace mantle. Granted, ninety-nine percent of orbs are airborne particulates, but this one was quite obvious. Given its proximity to the lit wall sconce above the fireplace, if it were dust or dander, it would have been drowned out by the lighting. Instead it appears to emit its own light energy while maintaining a transparent quality that allows the pattern of the curtain behind it to be visible through it.

The former hotel rooms upstairs are used mainly for storage and out-of-town family members who visit. When Bob's brother, Steve, was alive, he occupied one of these rooms. Steve described seeing a swirling, smoky energy manifesting in his room. While it made the hair on the back of his neck stand on end, he did not fear it. In other rooms, guests have reported seeing a young black man standing at the foot of the bed.

The Ladies' powder room opposite the kitchen and just outside the main dining room is credited with its own paranormal apparition of sorts. Bob said for about three consecutive weeks this "ghost buster" was taking pictures of the crack in the wall of this bathroom. This gentleman was supposedly capturing beams of light being emitted from this crack in the wall. I cannot attest to the validity of this claim as I did not see the photos. Additionally, I am not aware of the conditions under which he was "investigating" in terms of his equipment, his baseline, and variables such as moon phase, sun spots, etc. I took several photos of this crack with my Nikon digital camera at 16 mega pixel and did not capture any such anomalies.

We proceeded to the garden room and veranda, which were constructed about twenty-five years ago. Bob explained how careful he is to inspect these rooms before closing each night to make sure the candles on each table are extinguished. One night after completing this inspection and closing, he saw one of the table candles lit while in his car exiting the parking lot. He turned the car around and went back inside and blew the candle out once more. This particular candle has relit itself a couple of times since then, and, therefore, Bob makes it a point to do an additional visual check from the parking lot each night.

One night, shortly after closing at around 2:20 a.m., Bob was sitting at the bar with the chef. The bartender had just left to go to the kitchen. Bob heard one of the aluminum chairs in the veranda slide back from a table. He said it was a loud and distinct sound that he cannot replicate now since those chairs have been replaced with cast iron ones. Bob dashed to the veranda worried that someone might have jimmied open the door to swipe a bottle of whiskey, just like the month before. The bartender heard the chair move as well while he was in the kitchen. He ran down the front steps to the veranda while Bob ran down the side steps. They convened only to find the doors securely locked and no chairs moved away from any of the tables.

Kelly Mulrooney, a waitress, was kind enough to tell me of her ghostly experience that took place in 2014. She was waiting a late table. It was about midnight when the diners finally left. By 1:00 a.m., Kelly was cleaning the table and getting ready to shut down the main dining room for the night. She heard a chair slide behind her as if someone was there helping her and pushing the chairs in properly. She turned around to thank this "helper," but no one was there. Her manager was in the tavern with the bartender and the cooks had left for the night, so no one was in the kitchen. She was all alone.

She was disturbed by this incident, but then dismissed it and continued with closing up the dining room. She went to the parlor to make sure the lights were out, and they were. As she started back to the main dining room, she remembered she had not checked the deadbolt on the building's former front door. She turned around, and as she approached the front door, she could see the knob of the lock was pointing towards the right by about forty-five degrees. She knew in order for it to be fully locked, the knob would be straight up and down, or perpendicular to the floor. Before she could reach the knob to twist it to the locked position, an unseen hand corrected the knob right in front of her. She wondered if it were possible for the lock to right itself, but then the overwhelming chill consumed her, and she resolved to make a hasty exit for the night.

Bob is a credible witness in that he does not take every sound to be paranormal in nature. He does his due diligence in determining the cause of sounds heard in the restaurant. For example, several times he heard a loud crash come from inside the kitchen. It sounded like one of the pizza trays hitting the floor. He would inspect the kitchen, but not find anything amiss. He finally determined that one of the filters in the air vents above the stove would crash down after he turned off the exhaust fan. It wasn't immediate, though. It took a few minutes for the loss of air pressure from the fan being shut off. Then the filter would loosen and fall down behind the stove.

I interviewed a former hostess of the Tannersville Inn, Maureen Cunningham. Working there about twenty years ago, she detailed for me how she was by herself one night in the main dining room straightening up the room in preparation for closing. She heard a female voice from behind her distinctly. It said: "Hey Mo!"—which is her nickname. She turned around to greet the woman, but no one was there. Her arms became coated with goose bumps and she decided that was enough straightening up for that night, and she left. Maureen pointed out to me the goose bumps on her arms after telling me this experience. "Twenty years later, and it still affects me like this. That's how real and unnerving that voice was to me," she said.

As for the identities of the ghosts at the Tannersville Inn, that is still to be determined. Bob said some people suspect the inn's former owner, Mabel, who was in her eighties at the time she sold it to his family. She had been at the helm there for eighteen years.

One customer asserted that the ghostly presence of Jimmy Hoffa was at the inn. Bob laughs that off. "The spirits here may

Bob Jakubowitz, co-owner, by fireplace in main dining room—same room he saw the shadow fly by.

leave you feeling 'creeped out' at the time of their encounter, but you never feel overwhelmed or frightened out of your wits. There is an overriding sense of positive energy here," Bob explained.

I enjoyed the investigation at the Tannersville Inn even though I did not collect any EVPs (electronic voice phenomena). The cold temperature in the ladies' powder room was not paranormal, just the heat to that particular room had been turned down low. The photos were all "normal" save for the one possible orb in the parlor. Mabel, however, may be to blame for the disappearance of this chapter's printout and the publicity release form I dropped off to Bob to review and sign. I went back to retrieve the items from him a week later. He could not find them, and he knew for sure that he had placed them in the drawer of the antique dresser. Well played, Mabel, well played.

CHAPTER 2

Mauch Chunk
Opera House

Shadows, whispers, and more pervade this old theater.

The Mauch Chunk Opera House, pronounced "mock chunk," is at 14 West Broadway in Jim Thorpe, Pennsylvania. The building is owned by the Mauch Chunk Historical Society; Dan Hugos has leased and operated the theater since 2003. However, the theater first opened in 1882—after only eight months' construction time. Originally, the first floor served as a general store and food co-op, and the second floor housed the theater.

By 1925, a movie chain from Buffalo, New York, purchased the building and made it a focal point for entertainment. This was easily achieved since, by that time, Mauch Chunk was a key stop for the trains departing Penn Station in New York City to Buffalo with the eventual tourist destination being Niagara Falls. Popular entertainers of that time, such as Al Jolson, Mae West, and John Phillips Souza, headlined at the theater. Sadly, when oil replaced coal for heating, the town and this theater fell off the map. For a while, the building housed a purse manufacturer.

Today, the second floor has been scaled back to make a balcony, and the first floor has had leg-roomy seats installed. The view upwards from the first floor is about three stories.

Upon my arrival at the theater, I was greeted by Steve Hlavka, general manager. He was able to pronounce my maiden surname properly since he too suffered from the silent "H" at the start of his surname. Steve introduced me to Dan Hugos, the owner of the theater. Dan proceeded to take me on a fascinating, historical tour of the theater.

As we walked into the theater, Dan told me about the television show *Psychic Kids* was filmed there in 2012. The "psychic kids" sensed a spirit almost immediately upon entering the theater. They pinpointed the energy or spirit to be up behind the balcony, specifically the projection room. Dan said that it was supposedly the ghost of the former projectionist. However, no *definitive* information as to the identity of the spirit was determined.

Dan has heard many times from various people that someone fell from the scaffolding and died during the theater's construction. This poor soul may still be earthbound to the theater.

We went upstairs to the projection room. The view through the window where movies used to be projected through was quite impressive. In spite of my fear of heights, I managed to climb the fold-down ladder to

Dan Hugos, owner, (right) and Steve Hlavka,
manager (left).

investigate the attic. Dan pointed out the solid
construction of that time period. The ceiling vent was
installed in 1925 and still functions. Dan said: "We use
this in the warmer weather. The doors of the theater
seal much better than the original ones and when this
fan is activated, you can really feel the breeze generated
by the ceiling vent."

I asked Dan about his ghostly encounters or experiences at the theater. Shrugging his shoulders he said:
"For the most part, I haven't had any. I guess I'm just not
in the loop where that sort of thing is concerned." But
he did recall an odd feeling he had while working late.
He said it was probably around 3:00 a.m., and he was
painting the floors after the old seats had been removed

in preparation for the arrival of the new seats to be installed. He felt as if someone was looking over his shoulder. He turned around to look, but didn't see anyone. Even though he dismissed the feeling as being the product of his imagination and his body's need for sleep, he decided to pack up and leave rather quickly. Two months later, an eighty-five-year-old performer was at the theater doing a Chopin recital. Since he preferred to rehearse extensively prior to his performance, he was in the theater alone late at night. Subsequently, he confided to Dan that he experienced this uncomfortable presence lurking over his shoulder. It was so unsettling for him, that he ceased rehearsing and left the theater.

I recorded for forty-five minutes while in the theater, and did not capture any EVPs. Of course, Steve's ghostly howling of "Boo!" in the background of my recording while going up the stairs with Dan to the balcony proved quite humorous upon playback. While my photos captured typical dust orbs, my sense is that there is more going on here than what is performing on the stage. An encore investigation is certainly warranted at the Mauch Chunk Opera House.

CHAPTER 3

Sorrenti's Cherry Valley Vineyards

Great wine, great pizza, great ghosts!

Dominic and Mary Sorrenti purchased the 200 acres that comprise the vineyards and winery in 1981. By 2010, they sold 187 acres to the Cherry Valley National Wildlife Refuge. Their son, Nicholas, has added to the success of the winery by crafting award-winning wines—over 100 awards to date. While the wines created here are known for their flavor, it is the other spirits that make this winery all the more tempting to a ghost hunter or paranormal enthusiast.

I stopped in on a Sunday afternoon and was disappointed that I had just missed meeting Mary. However, the young lady I chatted with, Nicole, had some interesting experiences of her own to relay. She directed my attention to an angel-shaped wine stand. She said: "One day I was sitting there at the register with my back towards that wine display stand. All of the sudden, the bottle and the glass that were both adhered to the stand via a suction cup flew right past my head!" Donna, the other cashier, confirmed the near-miss of that day. She told me how she heard something and turned and saw the bottle literally fly right by Nicole's head, narrowly missing her.

Donna continued to tell me her experiences since working at the winery. She said the bottles in the storage facility "fall" off the shelves. She assured me that it's not faulty shelf construction or vibrations from people slamming doors. Additionally, Donna has fallen victim to the occasional practice of the Watermelon Rosé that is inexplicably rung up on that same register where Nicole was sitting when the bottle and glass flew past her. She explained: "I'll be ringing up an order, and I hit total, and when the receipt prints out, there's the Watermelon Rose printed on it along with the items I actually entered. Granted, it's a great wine, but it causes a ton of problems when the customer didn't purchase it and requests that the sale be voided and re-rung."

Nicole told me about their resident ghost "Henry," who is playful with his opening of doors. Of course with the harsh winter temperatures, the amusement fades quickly.

The sad story of Henry as relayed to me by John Hotchkiss and Mary Sorrenti is as follows: Supposedly, he was a farmer who treasured his animals. One night his barn caught fire and he could not rescue any of the animals. He was so distraught over their deaths, he hanged himself in the charred remains of that very barn. It makes for a great tale, but it could not be validated in historical records. What was found is as follows: Charles Saylor, who came from Germany, is the namesake of the Village of Saylorsburg. His son, Theodore, became Post Master of Saylorsburg, and his son, Charles Saylor (born in

Bright spirit orb captured on Dead End ramp along Route 33.

1807), built a large hotel in 1847 that he operated for nineteen years. He was also elected to the position of justice of the peace and held this title for thirty years. Other family ties include Edward Saylor, who was born in 1851 in the Lake House. Edward was a farmer and owner of a tannery and saddlery business. I could not find any lineage mentioning Henry.

The winery's sign can be seen from the Route 33 highway. In fact, this highway was installed to expedite travel from the Easton-Bethlehem areas to the Stroudsburg area in 1959, but wasn't completed until 1972. It cuts through what was once Indian burial ground, specifically Lenni-Lenape Indians. Patrons of the winery have reported hearing the ghostly screams and cries of the Indians' spirits.

Kent, my husband, and I took a nighttime walk up the deserted ramp that is alongside Route 33 and across from the winery. We attempted to capture EVP, but the whirling sounds of cars and trucks passing by on the highway and the wind made that close to impossible. As we climbed this ramp, the "low battery" warning flashed on Kent's camera. As a trained paranormal investigator, he knows to load fresh batteries in all the equipment before leaving for an investigation. Typically, when a spirit is near, they tend to drain the battery power in the equipment, such as cameras, camcorders, and audio recorders. A possible explanation for this phenomenon is that it is akin to an adrenaline rush for the ghost.

As we continued up the ramp, I captured several orb pictures, but one stood out in that the orb itself was giving off its own light. Since I dismiss ninety-nine percent of orbs as airborne particulates, I was intrigued with this one highly illuminated orb. Concurrent with the taking of this photo, I was recording for EVPs. I asked for a name after capturing this suspicious orb, but did not get a response.

Interview with John Hotchkiss

I was fortunate to interview John Hotchkiss, co-founder and director of the Coalition Offering Research Ethics C.O.R.E. Phenomena (CO.R.E.). He and his team investigated the winery, its basement, the barn, the farmhouse, and the one-room schoolhouse between May and June 2013.

John maintains that the barn was built on the same space as the one that burned down on Lower Cherry Valley Road and is practically a replica of the original. This space is used to store the wine-making equipment. The odors are strong given this equipment, but he and his team did detect the scent of cigars. Of course, no one on his team was smoking during the investigation. C.O.R.E. Phenomena follows similar protocols of the NJ Ghost Hunters Society wherein smoking during an investigation is prohibited as it may result in a false-positive ectoplasmic mist or vapor.

While conducting an EVP session, John asked: "Henry, if you're here, will you talk with us?" Suddenly, his teammate, Megan, was holding the K2 Meter and it lit up concurrently with the hair on her arms standing on end. Typically, the K2 is used by ghost hunters to demonstrate paranormal activity by its ability to light up using any combination of five small lights in the presence of EMF (electromagnetic field) spikes. Generally, it is calibrated at 60 Hz, but can detect EMF frequencies in the range of 30 Hz to 20,000 Hz. Therefore, it is best to power down other equipment, such as cell phones and two-way radios, when using the K2 to ensure it is reading ghostly EMF and not man-made EMF.

Megan of C.O.R.E. Phenomena Research using the K2 meter in the former barn.

The schoolhouse is on land that was originally Lenni-Lenape land. It is reported that the ghost of a Native American has been seen peeking in the windows of the schoolhouse and roaming the property. The schoolhouse windows today are boarded up. However, John has walked up the tract of land that Mary Sorrenti has since sold off, and he found rock pile formations consistent with those of Indian burial mounds. He also noted while walking in this area that it's like being in a bubble. One can hear the traffic of Route 33 and surrounding chaotic sounds of civilization, but there is this overwhelming sense of peacefulness.

Mary Sorrenti told John that she had seen little white, wispy "twisters" coming down the mountain in this area of the burial grounds. She maintains that the schoolhouse is the most active in terms of Indian spirit activity. While investigating the schoolhouse, they did capture orbs in pictures, but that's easily discounted given the dust.

In the café, otherwise known as the farmhouse, at approximately 2:30 a.m., John and his team captured on the night cams the sound of footsteps rushing across the floor above them. These footsteps were followed by a deliberate door slamming sound. Atypical of a residual haunt, they not only heard it, but recorded it. John tried debunking it by reasoning it was a truck going by on Route 33 creating the booming sound of rushed footsteps. However, this could not explain the door slamming sound.

Interview with Mary Sorrenti

After several failed attempts, I finally got to meet and interview Mary Sorrenti. She told me that Lorraine Warren, famous psychic medium who worked with her husband, Ed Warren, self-proclaimed Demonologist, on the Amityville Horror case, visited the winery a few years ago. Mary asked Lorraine: "What do you see here psychically?" Lorraine replied that she saw "wheels of energy." Mary interpreted these as the little white tornadoes.

The Indian energy is prominent on the property, according to Mary, especially over at the schoolhouse. She said a former paranormal group that investigated there captured an EVP of a straining voice saying: "Katahdin." This could relate to Mount Katahdin in Maine—the start of the Appalachian Trail. This trail is accessible from the winery property. As for the word "Katahdin," Mary said the investigative team contacted a Native American chief in one of the Dakotas who specializes in Native American languages. He explained that "Katahdin" was for the Lenni-Lenape a warning device to keep young children close to the camp and prevent them from wandering. A local historian told Mary that Cherry Creek was the water source that provided for the estimated 5,000 Lenni-Lenape Indians who lived on the property and neighboring land.

Mary recalled the time she saw a strange orange glow on the side of the mountain that looked like the face of a Native American princess. "I was driving my car, heading to the winery, when I noticed this strange orange glow. I slowed my car down to a crawl and realized the face of an Indian princess as if it was imprinted on the side of the mountain," Mary explained. Sometime after this experience, an older couple who were hiking on the Appalachian Trail came into the pizzeria and said: "We just had a strange experience up on the hill behind your place here." Mary could tell they were visibly shaken. They went on to say that, as

Old Schoolhouse where the ghost of a
Lenni-Lenape is seen looking in the windows.

they were hiking, they came to a spot where all the sounds were
silenced and they could not move. Some type of force was holding
them captive via paralysis. Once released from this grip and able
to hear the sounds of what was around them, they raced down
the hill to the first place they could find to ask for help—Sorrenti's
Winery. Mary gave them directions to East Stroudsburg University
as they requested. They wanted to get to the university as fast
as they could to research their experience to find an explanation
for it, and possibly, discover if others had had this experience
on that part of the trail.

Mary's friend came to do a cleansing years ago. Native
Americans call this a Smudging. Using a white sage wand the
smoke is passed around the home and property to rid the negative
energy and raise the vibrations to a more positive level. While
Mary drummed in the gazebo, her friend walked about the
property with the burning smudge wand. Suddenly, a vortex or
white tornado-like manifestation appeared and stormed around
the property and the gazebo. Mary said the force of this vortex
actually blew her and her friend's hair upwards as it passed by
them. Once it was gone, the smell of cedar wood was overwhelming.
Both Mary and her friend could smell it distinctly.

The Indian energy is one aspect of the paranormal energy present at the winery, according to Mary. She said the other aspect is Henry—the ghost who stomps across the second floor of the pizzeria and slams the door. Mary has heard these footsteps on several occasions. She noted: "They were so strong that I thought my husband was upstairs pounding across the floor. But then I remembered I was alone in the building."

Mary's grandson remarked to me that he has heard these footsteps and door slam on occasion while working in the pizzeria. He also mentioned the mischievousness of the ghost, citing the time an entire tray of items cleared from dining tables was on a table awaiting the journey to the dishwasher. After having sat on top of that table for two hours or more with no incident, it flew off the table and crashed to the floor. Mary's grandson witnessed the entire episode. A waitress heard the crash and turned to see what happened. She explained that there was no way for that tray to slip off the table. It had to have been pushed, but no one was near the table.

A deadly physical characteristic plagues the winery in the form of Route 33. The overpass for this highway abuts the winery's property. Because of the steep downgrade of the highway and rather tight bend, fatal accidents have occurred. Mary said: "We've pulled people from their cars." Mary explained her theory as to why this is such a high-traffic accident area of this highway: "The semi-tractor trailers misjudge this grade and bend in the road, causing them to end up in the other lane thereby forcing whatever vehicle that was in that lane off the road completely." Mary witnessed the horrific accident of a car "leaping" from Route 33 and crashing onto her property. She tried to tell the driver to stay still while she called 9-1-1, but his head injury made him delirious and he took off on foot for Route 33. He made it across the highway—all four lanes, and then, for some unknown reason, he turned to come back across the highway towards the winery. By the time he entered the second lane; he was hit head on by a fire truck and killed instantly. Mary said the scene was so gruesome that she had to send one of her employees for counseling afterwards as she was so upset.

Conclusion

26

Sorrenti's Cherry Valley Vineyards is a must-visit destination when in Saylorsburg. The wood-fired oven that bakes the best pizza to perfection and the award-winning wines and amazing sangria are reasons enough. For the ghost hunter, though, the para-energies abound and provide many opportunities for investigation.

CHAPTER 4

The Buck Hill Inn

*This abandoned former resort
is home to legends,
Native American energies,
and a vortex!*

What was once the prime place to vacation in the Poconos is now in ruins. The original twenty-room structure was built by the Quakers in 1901 as a mountain retreat. It expanded twenty-five years later to a four-story hotel with a total of 270 guest rooms. In 1981, Jacob and Astrid Keuler purchased the property and expanded it to 400 guest rooms. The Buck Hill Inn was considered a premier convention center, complete with a Donald Ross-designed golf course. However, ten years later, the Keulers closed the inn. Mrs. Keuler was hospitalized around this time, but she was not committed to an insane asylum as was rumored. In fact, she died in 1996 at the age of sixty-six while in the care of Laurel Nursing Center of Hamburg, Pennsylvania. Her husband, Jacob, died two years later.

As of October 1, 2015, the property was auctioned online, and the winning bid was $750,000. The winner of the auction has not, at this time, been disclosed. It has been rumored that the property is to be developed as part boutique hotel and part condominiums. "No Trespassing" signs are posted at every possible entry point, and it is best to heed their command. A local law enforcement friend of mine said that close to 400 trespassers at the Buck Hill Inn have been arrested.

I spent a week here with my grandmother back in the 1970s. Gram and I would start the day with breakfast in the dining room. She liked to linger and chat with her friend who was also visiting with her grand-daughter. I would get bored and wander to the conservatory. There was a beautiful grand piano there, and I would amuse myself by plunking out indiscernible tunes. Eventually, Gram would collect me, and we would return to our room to get ready for the pool. While I was taking swimming lessons, Gram would read the paper and chat with her friend.

Later, we would return to our room to change into more formal clothes to attend dinner in the dining room. This is also where I learned how to navigate a complicated place setting. Gram was patient and instructed me to "work from the outer utensil to the one closest to the plate with each course." Overall, my recollection of the inn is one of grandeur similar to what was depicted in the flashbacks Jack Nicholson's character had in the movie *The Shining*.

To see the remains of this hotel today is both sad and foreboding: part of it destroyed by fire, part of it crumbling, and the surrounding grounds are completely overgrown.

The inn was featured on the now-defunct MTV television show *Fear*. I was fortunate enough to interview Kelly and John

The beautiful stone gateway of the Buck Hill Inn.

Weaver who were involved with the episode that featured the Buck Hill Inn in March 2001. I first worked with Kelly and witnessed her amazing psychic ability in 2006 when she and John came to the New Jersey Ghost Hunters Society Ghost Conference that was held in Hackettstown, New Jersey. The conference attendees were invited to participate in an investigation of the Washington Theater in Washington, New Jersey. Kelly was instrumental in detecting several spirits during this investigation.

I found the particular episode of *Fear* on YouTube, and I was shocked when I saw Kelly billed as "Town Historian." John told me that to this day they do not know why they titled Kelly that way. Their inquiries have not been answered.

Kelly and John did their investigation of the inn in August 2000, a month before the show was filmed. The segment's production coordinator, his assistant, and a cameraman interviewed and filmed Kelly for over three hours while John documented findings via EMF (electromagnetic field), photography, and videography. Kelly insisted on not being told any information pertaining to the inn prior to her arrival. She was a "clear channel" with absolutely no preconceived ideas of the place.

Her first impression was the vision of a man being beaten to death in the tunnels that connect the buildings underground. It was later confirmed that a former security guard for the hotel detailed how a man's body was discovered brutally beaten to death in the very spot Kelly had her impression. It is suspected this murder was the result of a large gambling debt owed to the mob.

On the show, room 354 was where newlywed Lorna Kilpatrick was murdered by the very priest who performed her marriage ceremony two days prior. The priest committed suicide shortly thereafter. It was also disclosed that a maid named Monique Welton committed suicide in the bathtub by slitting her wrists and was found with her rosary beads in her cold, dead hands. The show never gave a time period for Lorna, but they mentioned August 1964 for Monique. When Kelly entered this room, she retreated quickly. She sensed an intense negative energy and was being told to get out.

When the hotel was in operation, guests reported an extreme cold in this room, the doors would not stay shut, and there was an uneasy, unwelcoming feeling in it. Maids were supposedly afraid to go in there alone to clean it. Eventually, the hotel stopped booking the room.

John Weaver captured a very bright orb on 35 mm film without using a flash in this room and he noted a sixteen degree drop in temperature on his thermal scanner. These reports coupled with Kelly's instant repulsion add up to the room being haunted. Whether it is an active or residual haunting remains to be determined. As for the stories of Lorna and Monique, well, I personally feel that the television show was very creative in its scare tactics. I searched every published copy of the *Daily Record* newspaper for August 1964. This was the newspaper for the Poconos at that time and the precursor to today's *Pocono Record*. There was no obituary for a Monique and no mention of the Buck Hill Inn or a suicide. I searched birth and death records back to 1901 for a Lorna Kilpatrick via the archives headquartered in Harrisburg, Pennsylvania. I found some Kilpatricks, but no Lorna Kilpatrick.

While in the library, a large room off the lobby and often referred to as "the lamp room," Kelly sensed that spirits were going in and out of a vortex. (A vortex is a type of portal or doorway between realms.) She remembers feeling light-headed while near this vortex. In the basement, there were tunnels, and she sensed mob activity in terms of people being beaten. Kelly said that overall the Buck Hill Inn has a negative energy and that no one could pay her enough to spend the night in the place.

I interviewed Christina about her experiences at the inn. Around 1998, as a teenager, she remembers driving around the abandoned hotel late at night with her friends. They all saw a light turn on in one of the windows, and while trying to make sense of it, she had to swerve the car to avoid hitting a deer in the road. Further down the road, a yellowish, slimy "blob" smacked onto the windshield. She said using the wipers only spread the substance across the window, making it impossible to see. She had to pull over and wipe the mess off the windshield with paper towels and napkins that she, luckily, had handy in the car. This perplexing and frightening experience only increased her fascination with the inn.

Christina wanted to test the local lore of the inn's "ghost cop." She explained: "Supposedly, if you encounter this ghost security guard or cop, he will advise you to leave the premises, but if you throw a rock at him, he disappears." Although she never did get to test this legend, she did get to tour the inn when it was open as a haunted house attraction in 2001. She said the "Lamp Room" had a dizzying negative energy to it. Christina said she could feel temperature fluctuations throughout the building, but it was definitely colder in the "Lamp Room."

I mentioned Kelly's impression of that room having a vortex, and Christina agreed stating: "It was like being in a downward spiral. I got nauseated from it."

We talked about the MTV *Fear* show filmed at Buck Hill. Christina said she heard that one of the female contestants in that episode took the rosary beads with her back to her native New York. Later the girl claimed to have been choked by the beads. She returned them to the hotel and sued the show, which led to its cancellation.

While there was a rumor that the show was canceled due to a death of one of the contestants, research proves otherwise. The show was canceled simply because of high production costs and low ratings. No contestant died during its production and the show was not sued by any former contestants.

Is the Buck Hill Inn haunted? Probably, but I cannot provide proof as gaining access is legally impossible. However, given the Native American land it's built on, the ninety years of active hoteling, and curiously abrupt closing, it's a safe bet that at the very least residual energies remain—that for some can be interpreted as ghosts. This is a "to be continued" chapter of this book meaning I'll have to wait and see what becomes of the property via its new owners.

CHAPTER 5

The Pocono Indian Museum

*Visit with the ghost of a
little boy and gentleman.*

As mentioned, one of the Indian tribes indigenous to the Poconos was the Lenni-Lenape. The tribe dates back to the New Jersey, eastern Pennsylvania, and Delaware areas approximately 10,000 years. According to the Nanticoke Lenni-Lenape website, Lenni-Lenape means "Men of Men" and is translated to mean "Original People." While the Lenni-Lenape were a peace-loving tribe specializing in mediation for disagreements between other tribes, they were also warriors. They were revered by other tribes as "grandfathers" or "ancient ones." Early European settlers admired the tribe for its tenacity, diplomacy, and hospitality.

Whether you enjoy the study of Native Americans or history in general, the Pocono Indian Museum is a must-see on your trip to the area. Not only is the collection in the museum extensive, but the building itself houses quite a history. The mansion was constructed in 1840 by John Van Campen Coolbaugh. Its many incarnations include being a speakeasy during Prohibition, a major stage coach stop, a brothel, a safe house stop on the Underground Railroad, as well as a dormitory for Camp Sunny Brook. By 1976, Marge and Mal Law purchased the run-down property and created the year-round dual business of a museum and ski shop.

I stopped in the museum and had the pleasure of chatting with Lorraine one Sunday afternoon. She's been the manager of the museum for the past sixteen years. Lorraine explained that since the addition of the ski shop, the paranormal activity subsided. She said there used to be a very serene quality to the energy and now it is void. However, her experiences over the years are well worth relaying.

Lorraine used to experience a tugging of her shirt at her waist. I told her that was indicative of a child given the height. She confirmed that one of the ghosts present in the gift shop is that of a child, a boy named Daniel as determined by a psychic medium who paid a diagnostic visit previously. The psychic felt that Daniel was a seven-year-old boy whose cause of death could not be discerned. Daniel was the son of one of the "ladies of the evening" in the brothel days. According to the psychic, his mother died in childbirth and Daniel was raised by the other ladies. Lorraine said this revelation explained why when she would open up the shop she would discover toys on the floor in front of the mirror as if someone had been playing with them. She knew for a fact that the floor was clear and toys were neatly placed on the shelves when she'd left the night before. What gives this psychic credence is the fact that she mentioned the location of the toys being in front of the mirror. Lorraine said there is no way she could have known that as it was never mentioned or discussed in the time the psychic was at the museum. The psychic went on to say that Daniel enjoys licorice. Therefore, at closing time, Lorraine tested to see if this were true by leaving black licorice in front of the mirror where Daniel would play with the toys. The next morning, the licorice was gone and the toys were in front of the mirror once more.

Daniel likes to celebrate his birthday, the psychic related further. While this in and of itself is not proof-positive of stellar psychic ability, what happened after this disclosure is. Lorraine said a mother and her daughter were visiting the museum. When they were leaving, the young girl stopped at the Indian mannequins seated at the entrance. She was looking right between the two mannequins and said while waving: "Good-bye Daniel! Happy birthday!"

The other ghost present at the museum is "Eli." Lorraine said that Eli was described as a tall, slender man with gray hair wearing a white shirt and black pants by the same psychic who detailed about Daniel. This description was confirmed by a woman visitor to the museum. She came to the counter and told Lorraine that she was nervous while touring the museum as there was this man following her. Lorraine said: "There is no man here. I'm the only one working today and you went into the museum alone." However, the woman was not comforted by these words and went on to describe the man exactly as the psychic had described "Eli." Lorraine did not have the heart to tell the woman that she had actually seen one of the museum's resident ghosts as the woman was clearly shaken up enough already.

Lorraine said prior to the addition of the ski shop, there was more room upstairs and they had tables and chairs for people to relax while perusing the many books they had for sale. One day, a lady came to the register to pay for her book selections and mentioned how this nice, older man helped her put all the books back on the shelves. The woman's description of the man fit that of Eli perfectly. Again, Lorraine knew better than to say that she and this customer were the only two living people in the place at that time.

The psychic said that she felt Eli was a caretaker of the property at some point in its history and aided the slaves using the Underground Railroad here. There is no documentation to support or validate the existence of "Eli" or "Daniel," but the non-psychic "everyday Joe" encounters and their descriptions give one reason to pause and consider both ghosts as viable. It's best to visit with black licorice on hand just in case you meet with Daniel and want to wish him a "Happy Birthday."

CHAPTER 6

Inn at Jim Thorpe

Poltergeist activity is evident in certain rooms.

e Pocono

Situated on the main drag of Jim Thorpe, 24 Broadway to be exact, is the Inn at Jim Thorpe. The original structure was known as the White Swan Hotel when Cornelius Connor opened for business in 1833. Sadly, his hotel burned down during the "Great Fire of 1849." He built another on the same land, calling it the New American Hotel shortly thereafter. During the late 1800s, the town of Mauch Chunk, Native American for "Bear Mountain," was second only to Niagara Falls for tourism. In fact, Mauch Chunk was a major stop on the train route from Penn Station in New York City to Niagara Falls. Notable guests of the hotel included General Ulysses S. Grant, President William Taft, and Thomas Edison.

The Great Depression hit the town hard and many residents left to find work and housing elsewhere. According to the inn's website: "The Inn fell into disrepair during the Depression, as Mauch Chunk, along with many of the region's coal towns, suffered from the economic downturn." Changing the name from Mauch Chunk to Jim Thorpe, in 1954, was the fortunate reprieve the town desperately needed.

In life, Jim Thorpe was a Native American who hailed from Oklahoma. He was an Olympic athlete (1912 record holder for the decathlon) and excelled in several sports: basketball, football, and baseball. His equestrian skills were far above average as well. In light of his accomplishments, and out of love for her husband, his widow wanted him honored post-mortem. His body was transported from Philadelphia to the newly dedicated town of Jim Thorpe. He is interred in a mausoleum on the east end of town.

Another fortunate event occurred in 1988 when David Drury purchased the structurally decrepit inn and restored it beautifully. Today, it provides the modern conveniences of Wi-Fi with the tasteful, elegant décor of the Victorian period. The second-floor porch with its ornate iron railing is reminiscent of the French Quarter hotels in New Orleans.

I met with Nancy Zeigler, public relations and marketing manager for the hotel. She was kind enough to lend me an all-access key for the hotel rooms on the list she devised from guest reports of peculiar or unsettling events they experienced while staying in these rooms. Melissa D'Agastino, my team leader for the Central Jersey Division of the New Jersey Ghost Hunters Society, and I set off to investigate each room on the list, knowing we would not be distracted or interrupted by anyone else. We asked that Nancy not disclose the reports to us prior to our investigation of the

Jim Thorpe's final resting place is on the east end of town.

rooms. We wanted to be completely unbiased in our approach to investigating each room.

Melissa and I decided to start out on the first floor and work our way up to the third floor. Room 104 is a quaint room next to an office. This location precluded any positive EVP capture given the background noise of the employees' meeting in that office. However, Melissa did detect a tugging on her pendulum. She asked: "Is there anyone here?" The pendulum began to circle in a counter-clockwise motion signifying "yes." It did not circle too long when it came to a stop, and Melissa noted that the heaviness she was feeling had lifted. There were no significant EMF spikes or temperature drops noted in this room.

We went to room 211 next. Supposedly this was one of the rooms of ill-fated lovers. The story detailed to David Drury by a psychic was that two lovers who were cheating on their spouses made plans to meet at the hotel. The woman checked into room 211 and the man checked into room 311. The failed rendezvous drove the woman to kill herself. Nothing of paranormal worth was captured in this room at the time of our investigation.

Room 303 is a suite complete with fireplace and Jacuzzi tub. While it's a very attractive room, we did not experience anything paranormal in here. The temperature held constant at sixty-six degrees, and no EMF spikes were detected. Upon review of the audio and video recordings from this suite, nothing was captured in the way of paranormal evidence.

Room 310 was our last stop on the list of rooms we were given. I was hopeful that by being across the hall from room 311 we would document some para-activity, but sadly that was not the case. Reports of the towels being disheveled in rooms 310 and 211 have been occurring since the 1970s according to Michelle Gallagher.

Upon returning to the lobby, we got to chat with Connie who works at the front desk. She has worked here since 2004. Shortly after she started, she had her first experience with the ghostly side of the business. She had the early morning shift and would arrive to start her day at 6:00 a.m. While she was prepping the front desk for her shift, she heard a man's voice come over the baby monitor calling out the name "Josephine." She explained that the baby monitors were used when she had to step away from the desk. She would take the monitor with her to to hear if a call was coming in to the front desk or if someone was ready to check in or out.

Connie also described a weird occurrence with the reservation system on the computer that occurred periodically. When logging in, the system date should default to the current day's date; however, sometimes a date in the late 1800s displays. She took a picture of the screen the last time this happened. Although she emailed me this picture, it is not a high resolution photo suitable for reprint in this book as it was taken with her cellphone. The date displayed on the screen that she photographed that day was *January 3, 1801*.

Nancy noted that the activity spiked about four years ago when they were renovating the restaurant. An employee, whose name is purposely withheld, told Nancy that one morning while setting up the continental breakfast she saw a ghostly figure of a woman just standing by the coffee maker. Nancy explained that this employee was skeptical when it came to all the ghost stories surrounding the hotel. Even though the employee saw the translucent woman by the coffee maker, and watched the ghostly female figure vanish from her sight, she could hardly believe it. Yet, she was bothered by it enough to not want to be alone that early in the morning thereafter.

Connie remembered she had another picture on her computer to show us. It was of a dresser in guest room 211 where one bottom drawer was open and the contents completely disheveled. The guest of the room who discovered this upon their return called the front desk to complain. Connie assured them that housekeeping would have had no reason to open the dresser drawer and rifle its contents.

While Melissa and I were packing up and getting ready to leave, Nancy added the story about the ceiling fans in the restaurant. These ceiling fans have the unique ability to spin and stop all by themselves—this is quite impressive when one considers that this start-and-stop motion occurs when the kitchen is closed and locked for the night. The kitchen is where the on/off switch for the ceiling fans is located.

My conclusion about the Inn at Jim Thorpe is that it's haunted regardless of the fact that I did not capture any evidence personally. The eyewitness accounts of employees and hotel guests are too much to dismiss. Therefore, I have added spending the night in Room 211 at this hotel to my ghost hunting bucket list.

CHAPTER 7

The Old Jail Museum

The handprint that cannot be removed from the cell wall and other ghostly sounds and impressions are waiting for you.

Sitting atop the crest of Broadway in Jim Thorpe, formerly known as Mauch Chunk, is the hand-cut stone fortress now known as the Old Jail Museum. It was built in 1871 as the Carbon County Prison and set partly into the rocky mountain so as to reinforce its lasting strength for incarceration. The jail had a warden's quarters occupying the front of the jail and its two stories. Until 1970, wardens and their families inhabited these rooms. After that, the space was repurposed for offices and storage.

The building was designed by architect Edward Haviland, who was the son of John Haviland, architect of the famous spoke-design of Eastern State Penitentiary in Philadelphia. The wrought iron fencing is crafted with an intricate rope design symbolizing, in effect, the very material that ended many convicted felons' lives. The jail has a total of forty-four confinement areas otherwise known as cells. Twenty-five cells are in the main cell block, and sixteen are in the basement, which is "the dungeon," and were used for solitary confinement of prisoners until 1980. The three remaining cells were allocated for women and located on the second floor. The cells measure eight feet by thirteen feet and the walls separating each cell are twenty-four inches thick. The front door to the prison weighs in at an impressive 1,000 pounds. The dedication sign carved in stone and affixed atop the front door contains the architect's name misspelled with two "L's" instead of one.

The gallows on display today are a re-creation of the original "Instrument of Death." This device was designed to efficiently and effectively hang four persons at one time. The positioning of the gallows is accurate with it being in the back end of the main cell block. Back in the day of executions by hanging, this placement allowed ample room for onlookers via the stairs, balcony of the second floor and, of course, the main floor of the cell block.

In January 1995, the last of the prisoners housed here were relocated to a new prison four miles away. Two weeks later, the former prison became the property of Tom and Betty Lou McBride. The couple worked diligently on the restoration of the prison and opened it as the "Old Jail Museum" in May of that year.

It was not long before tourists began approaching Tom, Betty Lou, or the tour guides with queries regarding the strange sensations experienced while inside the building. Betty Lou kept a file and would write the experience down along with date of occurrence. Approximately ten years later, Betty Lou compiled those notes into a book: *Ghosts of the Molly Maguires? A Decade of Strange & Unusual Happenings in the Old Jail.*

For one to have a full appreciation and understanding of the residual and possibly active haunting at this museum, I must address the history of the Molly Maguires.

Anthracite coal was big business for Mauch Chunk and its surrounding areas. The Lehigh Coal and Navigation Company was the local giant in this industry of mining. By 1861, the company owned and operated ten mines and was the founding force of the "community" comprised of close to 4,000 men, women, and children. Most of the miners were Irish immigrants. They worked long days in the mines and retired in the evenings to the houses they rented from their employer. The miners were expected to provide their own tools, such as picks and axes, to do their work and were at the mercy of the company store for food and supplies. To complete the control the company exerted over the miners, the men were paid in "company scrip," which was only accepted at the company's store with its inflated pricing structure. In many cases, after deductions from salary for rent, food, and supplies, miners actually owed the company. They were working to starve and go further into debt.

An average annual income for a miner was $300. At the time of the Civil War, $300 was the going rate to purchase a substitute or exemption from the government. The substitute went in the place of the man who was drafted. It simply was a lose-lose situation for the miners. They faced being killed in action; and, should they return safely after the war, they feared losing their jobs to the newly freed slaves who would be seeking employment.

Working conditions for miners were fraught with danger: cave-ins, floods, fires, etc. In 1868, the Workers' Benevolent Association was formed with the goals of achieving better wages and safer working conditions for the miners. While its initial relationship with the coal companies was functional, that cooperation and functionality quickly disintegrated within a few years and the WBA ceased to exist. The coal companies began to blame all their ills on a group they dubbed the Molly Maguires. In fact, the president of the Philadelphia and Reading Railroad, Franklin B. Gowen, wielded media power by insisting the name Molly Maguires be cited frequently in the newspapers thereby leading the public to believe in the existence of this Irish rebel group.

Gowen went on to hire a Pinkerton detective, James McParlan, to pose as "James McKenna" a miner. His job was to work alongside the suspected Molly Maguires, gain their trust, to learn their secrets, and then report back to Gowen. In fact,

Re-creation of the gallows used to hang four of the condemned Molly Maguires concurrently.

McParlan's testimony led to the conviction and execution of several supposed Molly Maguires.

The Ancient Order of Hibernians (AOH) was formed in 1836 to provide support and help to those Irish arriving in America. By 1872, Thomas P. Fisher, a known protestor and resister of the Civil War draft, became a county delegate of this order. Fisher agreed to represent the miners in talks with the Lehigh Wilkes Barre Coal Company in 1874. The miners' seven-month strike ended in July 1875, and two months later a mine superintendent, John P. Jones, was murdered. Three men were arrested for the murder: Alexander Campbell, Edward Kelly, and Michael Doyle.

Meanwhile, Charles Mulhearn, a miner who was found guilty of conspiracy to murder two brothers, admitted to participating in the murder of Morgan Powell, superintendent of the Lehigh Coal and Navigation Company in 1871, and implicated Fisher, John Donahue, Alexander Campbell, and Patrick McKenna. By June 21, 1877, Campbell, Doyle, Kelly, and Donahue were concurrently hanged on the specially designed gallows.

Thomas Fisher was arrested for the murder of Powell in October 1876 along with McKenna. The trial began in December of 1876. Fisher was not allowed to testify on his behalf. Also, the name Ancient Order of Hibernians was used interchangeably with the name Molly Maguires throughout the trial. This created the idea in the jurors' minds that if one was a member of the AOH, then one was a member of the Molly Maguires.

Ten days after the start of the trial, December 16, 1876, a verdict was rendered convicting Fisher of murder in the first degree and McKenna of murder in the second degree. McKenna was sentenced to nine years at Eastern State Penitentiary; Fisher was sentenced to death by hanging.

The next eighteen months Fisher spent in Carbon County Prison while his attorneys filed appeals. Unfortunately, Fisher was hanged on March 28, 1878. In his final words, he maintained his innocence and said he forgave those who had wronged him and hoped those he had wronged forgave him as well.

In my reading and research of these Molly Maguire trials and executions, I have concluded that fairness was not included in the trials. The gut-wrenching account of the 1879 hangings of Charles Sharp and James McDonnell for the 1863 murder of George Smith supports my conclusion.

January 13, 1879, the day before their scheduled execution, Sharp and McDonnell's lawyer went to Harrisburg, Pennsylvania, to seek clemency from Governor John F. Hartranft. With the governor being away on business, the lawyer was not able to secure a stay of execution until the morning of the hangings. He sent a telegram to Mauch Chunk and instructed the telegraph operator to rush this notice to the prison. In spite of the snow-covered, uphill jaunt, Philip Laudenslager, the telegraph operator, made it to the prison door minutes before the fatal floor fell from the gallows. He joined the wives of the condemned men with banging on the prison door and screaming for the sheriff to halt the execution in light of the telegram he had in his hands. It's estimated that he arrived at 10:41 a.m. Yet, Sheriff Raudenbush dismissed the increased banging and screaming as that of the wives and gave the order to proceed with the execution at 10:52 a.m. Tragic.

The Old Jail Museum is now home to energies that are rooted in depression and anguish. The traumatic experiences of executions and suicides have left their mark—in the case of cell number 17, quite literally. On one wall in this cell is the smudgy handprint of one of the hanged Molly Maguires. It is said that prior to leaving his cell for his march to the gallows, he rubbed his hand in the dirt of the cell floor and placed it on the wall to leave a print that would remain forever as a symbol of his innocence. The identity of this innocent man is not confirmed. Some believe it to be the handprint of Thomas P. Fisher, and others believe it to be that of Alexander Campbell, while others believe it is Michael Doyle's handprint.

In any event, the handprint is still there. It has been painted over many times throughout the years and always reappears. One attempt to rid the print involved chiseling off the plaster and re-plastering the wall. However, the print re-emerged.

When I interviewed local artist/psychic/shop owner, Michelle Gallagher, she told me that she dislikes having to park her car or walk anywhere near the Old Jail Museum because she "hears" tormented screams emanating from the former prison. She also experiences a physically sickening feeling when in front of the building and, therefore, has never made it inside. For Michelle, such a physical reaction translates to very dark and sinister energy and/or entities being present. She feels that the executions and suicides created a negative portal inside the jail.

When my Team Leader, Melissa D'Agastino, and I visited and investigated the Old Jail Museum in 2015, we had the place to ourselves save for its owners, Tom and Betty Lou McBride. The McBrides graciously signed my copy of their book and allowed Melissa and I to wander the jail and dungeon uninterrupted.

The famous handprint in Cell 17 is copyrighted and, therefore, I was not permitted to photograph it. I remained at the cell long enough to conduct an EVP session. Nothing was captured, though. The average temperature in the main cell block was fifty-four degrees. The howling wind outside the building made it difficult at times to do EVP work.

According to Betty Lou McBride's book, the key areas for paranormal experiences are Cell 17, Cell 6, the library, the laundry room, and the dungeon. Reports include being pushed in the library, hearing cursing while in the dungeon, having trouble walking in Cell 6, and hearing men in Cell 17.

The dungeon is famous for draining fresh new batteries in cameras—both digital and film. I experienced this drain on my Sony camcorder, which has a double-capacity battery that had 157 minutes of power left on it. Within minutes of entering the dungeon, the low battery symbol began flashing on the camcorder's screen. I continued to record in order to get as much as I could on digital video. Melissa's equipment, however, did not suffer any battery energy loss. My Nikon digital camera did not lose any battery power either. This apparent selective quality of power drainage is curious to me.

As a writer, I take comfort when in the company of books, such as a library. I went to the second floor of the prison and

The dungeon with questionable orb.

stood outside the library room. My normal feeling of comfort was nowhere to be found while staring into this dark room of dusty books on the shelves. Years ago the McBrides made the decision to cordon off the room as too many people were being pushed and shoved by unseen hands. I attempted to record for EVP and took some pictures while standing outside this room, but I could not remain there long enough to capture any evidence. It was an overwhelming and disturbing feeling and I had to leave the area.

I went to the opposite end of the second floor to secure a bird's-eye view of the gallows. I was able to breathe much easier in this area. I kept recording on my digital audio recorder, but upon review I had not captured a single EVP while in the Old Jail Museum. Melissa reviewed her recordings and had not captured any EVP either.

For twenty years, Betty Lou McBride has heard many paranormal testimonials from visitors, tour guides, and even local paranormal investigative teams. She has noticed some interesting similarities, such as women wearing the color purple tend to experience odd things while in the prison. Some have even seen the apparition of a woman in purple-colored clothing.

Men named "Tom" seem to be targets of ghostly interaction, and children, particularly those aged between ten and twelve, relate stories of feeling comforted and peaceful. Girls often report the feeling of a guiding hand resting on their shoulder in the dungeon. There have been times when visitors have seen a "woman in white" descending the main staircase in the cell block, or have heard a woman's voice saying: "Too late. I'm too late." And, finally, the olfactory system is not immune to the Old Jail's paranormal smells of rotten eggs or flowers.

To clarify, a paranormal smell or scent is one that is there long enough for one to discern what the smell or scent is and then it is gone. I've experienced this personally with the smell of pipe smoke while at the Spy House in Port Monmouth, New Jersey. No sooner did I think to myself that I would succumb to a migraine from the smell, it was gone . . . completely gone.

Having been to Eastern State Penitentiary many times over the years, I figured how scary could this little jail museum be—especially in broad daylight as it was when we visited. I couldn't have been more wrong. Granted, I did not capture any evidence in the way of EVP or full-body apparitions, but the "feeling" I had while standing outside the library cell still bothers me. Would I go back to the Old Jail Museum? You bet! The ghost hunter in me cannot resist.

CHAPTER 8

The Rain Man of Stroudsburg

The most bizarre and heavily eyewitnessed case to take place in the Poconos.

Stroudsburg is a charming town with its "Main Street USA" appearance of retail and antique shops, restaurants, and theater. Yet, one block over from Main Street is Anne Street. On Anne Street is where this terrifying story begins.

February 24, 1983, was the funeral for Mr. James Kishaugh. His grandson, Donald Decker, was released from the Monroe County Correctional Facility on a compassionate furlough for the weekend to attend the service. Donald was just twenty-one-years old and still painfully cognizant of the physical abuse his grandfather used to inflict upon him. Although Don was incarcerated at the time, it should be noted that it was for the receiving of stolen goods. He certainly was not on the FBI's "Most Wanted" list.

Donald remembers people being sad and expressing their good-byes at the funeral, but all he could feel was relief and, strangely, joy that this old man was dead and would never be able to harm him again. After the funeral, his own parents forbade him to stay with them, so he stayed with Bob and Jeannie Kieffer, friends of the family.

Bob sensed that Donald was sincere in wanting to finish serving his time, get out of prison, and turn his life around. Therefore, Bob opened his home to Donald for the weekend. Before dinner was ready, Donald went upstairs to the bathroom to wash up. The rest of the family was readying the dinner table.

While in the bathroom, Don noticed the air temperature dropped—there was a distinct chill. Suddenly, he felt a loss of control and fell to the floor. He saw the visage of an old man wearing a crown staring at him with a sardonic smile on his face through the bathroom window. Then he felt the tearing of his flesh on his forearm. Meanwhile, the family gathered at the dinner table, and they were waiting for Donald to join them.

The episode in the bathroom concluded and Donald was able to get himself up and to the bathroom sink. He saw three scratches on the underside of his forearm ending just before his wrist. He washed the blood from the wounds as best he could and buttoned his shirt sleeve at the wrist attempting to conceal the marks. He proceeded downstairs to join the family for dinner.

Bob noticed the scratches peeking out from Donald's shirt sleeve when Donald reached for his glass of water. Bob grabbed Don's arm and examined the scratches and inquired about them. Don told Bob what happened while upstairs in the bathroom. Bob could not offer an explanation. He was dumbfounded.

After dinner, the family and Donald gathered in the living room to watch television and relax. A loud noise was heard above them and the room began to get cold. Then, Jeannie notice water dripping down the wall and called Bob's attention to it. Bob approached the wall as more water began to stream down. He touched the "water" and described it as having a tacky or sticky consistency. The "rain" began to fall from the ceiling throughout the living room. Jeannie feared that they had a pipe burst, but Bob was quick to point out that there was no plumbing in this part of the house. He couldn't understand or explain what was happening. He called his landlord, Ron Van Why and begged him to come over. Bob did not want to share what was happening over the phone as it was too fantastic.

Ron and his wife, Romayne, arrived shortly thereafter and were just as perplexed by the situation, which at this point had increased to a "steady rain" throughout the entire room. Ron suggested going upstairs to check for leaks—even though it had not rained for the past several days. Bob was hesitant to go upstairs since Don had been attacked there before dinner, and now the family dog, which normally slept in that bathroom, was appearing fearful to even go near the stairs.

The two men ventured upstairs and inspected the bathroom sink and tub for leaks. None were found. However, they both felt the presence of something unnatural and evil. When they returned downstairs, they noticed Donald was in some state of trance—just staring blankly. Bob called police not knowing what else to do.

Officers John Baujan and Richard Wolbert arrived on the scene and witnessed the indoor rain that was not only falling from above them, but actually defying gravity and flowing up from the floor they stood on. Wolbert said the "water" was even traveling horizontally. The officers called their chief of police, Gary Roberts, to the house. Chief Roberts determined there was nothing more than a leaky pipe situation in progress and ordered the officers to leave and not file a report.

Jeannie took Donald to the pizza parlor around the corner from their home. Mysteriously, the rain inside the house stopped once Donald was removed. Once Jeannie and Donald were inside Pam Scrofano's pizzeria, the rain began to fall inside there as well. Pam was convinced that Don was possessed. She took the crucifix she kept in the register and placed it in Don's hand, and it burned him. With that, Jeannie took Donald back to her house. The rain in the restaurant stopped just as mysteriously as it had started.

Once back in the Kieffer house, the rain resumed falling indoors. Jeannie and Romayne confronted Don in the kitchen. As they begged him to make the rain stop, pots and pans in the kitchen began to clang together making a loud noise. Then, suddenly, Don was lifted by an unseen hand at his throat and hurled across the room crashing into the corner and landing on the floor. This impact broke Donald's trance-like state. As he struggled to get on his feet, he felt pain on his arm once more. This time the scratches were in a crown formation atop the previous scratches. The Kieffers and Van Whys were completely terrified.

Jeannie took out her Bible and began to read Psalms 23 hoping to calm Donald and release him from the grips of this demonic entity. Officer Baujan returned at this time as he felt he couldn't just leave the family like his chief ordered him to do. He witnessed the "rain" now concentrating on Jeannie as she read aloud from the Bible. She was drenched.

The next day, Officer Baujan returned with Lt. William Davies and Lt. John Rundle to check on Donald and the Kieffers. Like clockwork, the "rain" resumed falling inside the house. Lt. Davies placed a crucifix in Don's hand and it burned him just like the night before at the restaurant. However, this time Donald was levitated and hurled against the wall and scratch marks appeared on his throat.

Later that same day, Donald returned to prison. He noticed the guards' uneasiness around him. Apparently, the news of Don's weekend had traveled swiftly back to the prison. Once in his cell, it began to rain thereby scaring his cellmate. The warden opted to place Don in a cell of his own. It was here that two prison guards dared Donald to make it rain on the warden, whose office was on the opposite side of the prison from Don's cell. This time Don seemed in control, not "blanked out." He believed he had the power to make it rain on command. By rubbing his fingers together and meditating, he was able to soak the warden's shirt in the center of his chest—remarkable given the several locked doors and barriers between Donald and Warden Dave Keenhold.

Warden Keenhold was convinced that Donald was possessed and called Reverend William Blackburn, the prison's chaplain, to perform an exorcism. Donald was taken from his cell and brought to meet Rev. Blackburn in a room outside the cellblock. Once inside this room, the reverend took hold of Donald's hand and began to read from the Bible. Don noticed a foul odor forming in the room, like that of rotting flesh and it intensified as the reverend continued to read from his Bible. Then the rain came, only this time it was pelting the reverend—soaking him. Yet, his Bible remained dry. The rain, for some reason, did not touch the Bible. After some prayers and commands by the reverend to rid young Donald of this evil spirit, the rain stopped and the odor abated. The exorcism was successful.

Donald Decker's story appeared on the 1993 television show *Unsolved Mysteries* and on *Paranormal Witness* in 2011. While watching the latter show, I noticed Donald said at its conclusion: "nothing like that ever happened to me again."

And, fortunately, demonic possession never did happen again. Sadly, more trouble with the law did. In 2011, Dana's Restaurant and Tavern owner, Theodoros Kyriakopolous asked Don to set fire to his restaurant so that he could file a claim on the insurance. From that claim money, Theodoros would pay Donald $25,000. Feds ruled the fire as arson and Kyriakopolous went to jail for insurance fraud, and Decker turned himself in to federal court in Wilkes-Barre.

Decker's inability to be an arsonist does not take away from his 1983 possession. A total of nine eyewitnesses—six of whom were law enforcement—certainly lends credibility to such an incredible story. There are skeptics who contend that someone should have taken pictures or video of the rain phenomena. What one has to remember is that this was 1983, and the battle between VHS and Beta was in high gear. Most people did not own a VHS player let alone a handheld recorder. As for the police on the scene, they were trying to figure out the cause of the rain indoors. They were not thinking about taking pictures.

Personally, when I was a novice paranormal investigator, I missed the opportunity to take a picture of key poltergeist activity on a case in north Jersey. I came into the kitchen to find the chairs turned from the table and facing the chair across the kitchen that was turned from its desk and facing the table's chairs. It was reminiscent of the chair stacking scene in the 1982 movie *Poltergeist*. I confirmed that no one on the team or a family member had moved the chairs. Team members were in awe of the arrangement as well. We reset the chairs and set up a static camcorder in the kitchen and returned to the basement hoping the event would happen again and this time be caught on video. Not one of us thought to take a picture of what had just happened.

Donald Decker's weekend furlough in 1983 is a classic example of poltergeist activity. I have always defined poltergeist activity as more of a result of the living rather than the dead. When someone internalizes stress, they are holding in energy. And, once they are relaxed or relieved, that stress—or energy—manifests outwardly in the form of loud banging noises or objects hurling about the room. Children who suffer abuse internalize a tremendous amount of stress. Since they are physically too small to fight back against their abuser, they hold in their fear, anger, sadness, and pain. Once they fall asleep, that stress finds a way to launch a toaster at the abuser's head. Or it scares them into thinking the house is haunted because the lights are flickering on and off; and there's the sound of dishes crashing to the floor in the kitchen. Donald's grandfather physically abused him as a child. It is no wonder Donald felt a sense of relief—not grief—at the funeral. And true to form, that night is when the poltergeist activity started.

It is possible, though, that Donald's poltergeist activity was coupled with some demonic activity. In Judaic lore, there is the three-headed demon known as Asmodeus. Of his three heads, bull, ram, and ogre, the ogre is closest to what Donald described as the man's face in the window. Asmodeus is known for his powers of wrath and revenge and focuses on disrupting households—particularly causing trouble between spouses. Certainly that weekend saw trouble within the walls of the home and later within the walls of the prison—everywhere Donald was at that time. According to the book *A Field Guide to Demons, Fairies, Fallen Angels & Other Subversive Spirits*, in order to rid this demon, the heart and liver of a special fish known only to the angels must be placed on an incense burner and roasted. The sickening odor will drive the demon away. When Reverend Blackburn conducted his exorcism, Don reported the smell of rotting flesh becoming increasingly evident. Perhaps the angels were coming to the reverend's aid and burning that celestial incense?

The house the Kieffer's rented on Anne Street is no longer there. It was demolished years ago and the property converted to a parking lot for a nearby church. Donald Decker was a resident of Gouldsboro, Pennsylvania, when he turned himself for arson in 2011. Pam Scrofano's restaurant is long gone as well. But the lasting "sleep with the lights on" feeling that Don's story of demonic possession generates lives on to this day.

CHAPTER 9

The Shawnee Inn

Watch a lady in white stroll through the lobby.

The beautiful, sprawling Shawnee Inn is in the heart of the Delaware Water Gap area of the Poconos. Today, it is a massive resort inclusive of a playhouse and timeshare property. It is also home to a few ghosts who have not, as yet, checked out of the famous inn.

Dating back to the 1890s, it was originally the summer home to successful businessman and New Yorker Charles Campbell Worthington. Eventually, he made the summer home his year-round home and hotel known as the Buck Wood Inn.

In 1912, Worthington installed an eighteen-hole championship golf course designed by A. W. Tillinghast. "Tillie," as he was known, was responsible for many championship golf courses throughout the United States, including Baltusrol in Springfield, New Jersey. The Professional Golfers Association (PGA) traces its roots to the Buck Wood Inn. In fact, the PGA Championship was held at the inn in 1938.

The Buck Wood Inn was sold in 1943 to a company led by famous band leader Fred Waring. Waring and his Pennsylvanians recorded several songs. The most recognizable would be the 1927 song: "I Scream, You Scream, We All Scream for Ice Cream." Waring maintained the inn as a high-end seasonal resort and produced and broadcast his radio program from Worthington Hall at the inn.

Karl Hope purchased the inn from Waring in 1974 and went on to develop the timeshare portion of the property. Hope's vision was to make the inn enjoyable, and profitable, year-round. After hiring former Olympic gold medal skier Jean Claude Kiley and growing the ski resort portion of the inn, Hope sold the business to the Kirkwoods in 1977.

Charles and Ginny Kirkwood expanded the resort by adding a golfing school, miniature golf course, and driving range. Making use of the Delaware River, they added the "Shawnee River Adventures," which today includes rafts, kayaks, canoes, and fishing trips. Later, they added snow-making capability and renovated Worthington Hall to become the Shawnee Playhouse, which hosts several productions throughout the year as well as holiday specials such as *The Nutcracker* and Handel's *Messiah*.

The name of the property was changed in 1994 to The Shawnee Inn and Golf Resort. Today, it encompasses its own brewery, top notch spa, as well as the original high standard of dining, hoteling, and golfing. The resort also hosts several Pocono favorite events throughout the year, such as the Garlic Festival and the Wing Off—the best chicken wing competition. The views are stunning no matter what season one decides to visit here, and so is the ghostly activity.

I was fortunate enough to interview John Hotchkiss of the Coalition Offering Research Ethics (C.O.R.E.) a paranormal investigating organization headquartered in the Pocono region, but covers the Slate Belt and Lehigh Valley areas as well. In addition to his twenty-six years' experience as a paranormal investigator, John has investigated The Shawnee Inn on several occasions for the past three years. He and his team employ a high level of professionalism, adherence to scientific protocols, and ghost-hunting equipment. What I admire about John is his dedication to "para unity." He is committed to sharing the information and education with fellow ghost hunters rather than hoarding it.

In January 2014, John and his wife and paranormal investigative partner, Liza, were investigating the inn. While in the Delaware building, which is the former stable where twelve horses died in the flood of 1955, John witnessed the backside of an upper-torso apparition of a woman entering one of the rooms at the end of the hallway he was facing. Sadly, Liza had her back to John and her static camcorder was facing her vantage point of the hallway. John raced toward the room he saw the ghost enter, but found no one there. This was a classic example of the one that got away.

The Shawnee has its own "woman in white" story, too. John said that finding any formal information on this woman is near-to-impossible as the inn probably did not want the negative publicity, but her story has been handed down from employee to employee.

The story goes that around the time shortly after the stock market crash, two wealthy families based in New York City arranged a marriage for the one family's son to the other family's daughter. This union would have benefited the woman's family greatly in terms of recouping their wealth. The day of her wedding, the distraught bride went to her room, number 109, tied a rope around her neck, and hanged herself. She was found wearing her wedding gown, but not the veil. Over the years this "woman in white" has been seen walking down the main staircase, passing through the lobby and vanishing back towards the entrance to the ballroom. The interesting fact about this apparition when it occurs is that she is not seen as some filmy, gauzy ghost, but rather as solid as any living, breathing person. She doesn't speak or make any notable sound as she passes by the concierge desk on her way through the lobby and towards the hallway to the ballroom.

A few doors down from room 109 is room 105, the site of a murder. Again, finding any tangible news clippings on this story is impossible. Yet, John said the story centers around a couple arguing because the husband suspected his wife was cheating on him.

Room 307 has mirrors galore and it's suspected that spirits are using the mirrors as portals to come and go through. People have reported seeing figures walking in this room when they know for certain they are the only person in the room at the time. This room is located above the aforementioned haunted hot spots of rooms 109 and 105. John captured some ghostly faces in these mirrors using a full-spectrum camera. This is a digital camera that is capable of photographing within the entire color spectrum of light, from Ultraviolet (UV) to Infrared (IR). One particular night he and Liza were in this room and there was a terrible thunderstorm raging outside. John was taking successive pictures in the direction of the mirrors and noticed the one shot had a face with its mouth opened. He figured Liza moved while he took the picture and generated a different reflection of light from her face. So, he asked her to wave to him. When she did, he realized she was completely across the room and in no way impacting the photos he had taken with her image or reflection.

The night John's team was stationed in the ballroom conducting research on the woman in white, it was relatively dead in terms of paranormal activity. His one investigator was wearing headphones and recording for EVP. John asked aloud for the spirit to make some sort of indication that she was present, since they had been there for a few hours with no sign or contact whatsoever. He then said: "Would you like us to leave you alone?" Then, from the kitchen they all heard pots and pans crashing to the floor. John said it was not one crash, but several successive crashes. Then they heard boxes being tossed about. The investigator wearing the headphones had his ears blown out—it was that loud. The team ran to the kitchen and found several pots and pans on the floor and boxes in disarray—this was all in the area where she has been seen in the past. John inspected the shelves and realized they had a "lip" on the edge of them that would prevent a pot or pan from simply slipping off the shelf. These items had to be lifted and then hurled to the floor. Additionally, the pots and pans were flung from various shelves in a sporadic pattern. It was not a case where one pot fell and knocked the others off the shelf like a domino effect. He also noted that there was no other way in or out of the kitchen other than the way they'd gone in. They did not see anyone else in the kitchen, nor did they see anyone else leave the kitchen. John concluded that when a woman, living or dead, throws pots and pans around the kitchen, it's pretty clear she wants to be left alone.

One other night while investigating the ballroom, John and his two teammates felt a rush of energy as if something was charging directly at them. They were all wearing headsets and heard the "whoosh" sound independent of each other as the energy surged past them. Nothing was noted on the EMF meter or captured in terms of audio or video, but they all felt and heard that energy.

In 2015, John's team partnered with Bob Christopher of NEPA (Northeast Pennsylvania Paranormal Group) to investigate the Waring room at The Shawnee Inn. Bob is the "go-to-gadget-guy" of ghost hunting. He has designed and installed touch sensitive electronics inside lifelike looking stuffed dogs and cats. These stuffed animals are placed in a room in the hopes to draw out a spirit who was fond of such animals. If a spirit gets within two to three inches of the stuffed animal, its nose and collar light up. Bob also designed "domes" that measure the buildup of static electricity. He placed a dome in each of the four corners of the Waring room and within forty-five minutes, the dome in the back corner began to light up. As it faded, the dome in the front corner on the same side of the room began to light up. The teams could track, in a sense, the very movement of the spirit's energy in the room by watching which domes lit up and then faded. While this was happening, a team member collecting EVPs asked if the spirit wanted them to leave. The answer was recorded, clear as a bell: "No."

To sum up The Shawnee Inn and Golf Resort, I would say "haunted." Thankfully, nothing malevolent or negative resides here. Therefore, one can truly relax with a deep tissue massage in the spa while their significant other is perusing the ballroom for the Woman in White. Personally, I would opt for being up most of the night investigating, followed by a massage the next day to relieve the kinks in my neck from all that data review.

Lobby the Lady in White walks through on her way to the ballroom.

C.O.R.E. Phenomena group having a little ghostly fun at The Shawnee Inn.

CHAPTER 10

The Tom X Pub

Apparitions and appetizers are being served.

Ghosts of t

The Historic Tom X Pub in East Stroudsburg has quite a history and quite a share of ghostly tales to tell. According to their website: "its name came from an unidentified settler whose name was Tom, who was killed by Indians." The more accepted story is that of Tom Mix, a famous cowboy and movie star in the 1920s. He went on to make a reported 336 films between 1910 and 1935. All but nine of these films were silent. He was Hollywood's first Western megastar along with his horse Tony. He loved to spend money and is known to have been married five times (now that's a few X's!).

The night friends and I went to this pub for dinner, I was hopeful to interview the waitress my friend overheard, on a previous visit, talking about the ghosts of the pub. I truly lucked out. Not only did I get to interview that very waitress, but I had the best cheeseburger in the Poconos. Whether or not you're into ghost hunting, I suggest the Western Burger complete with BBQ sauce and jalapenos. It is delicious! Plus, I like my burgers well done and that means one of two results: not well done, or overdone and dry. Not the case with this pub's burger. It was cooked through—well— but still juicy.

The building dates back at least 100 years. The dining room sits above the original foundation. It is rumored that the basement served as a stop on the Underground Railroad and may even have served as a speakeasy during Prohibition. Like most buildings surviving a century, it had its brothel days as well.

The waitress's first experience with ghosts was when she was helping the owner paint the pub. When they took a lunch break, they decided to move one of the tables out to the closest parking space so they could sit and eat in the fresh air. The waitress glanced up at one of the windows of the attic, and saw a man's face appear as if he had walked up to the window, turned, and walked away. She mentioned this to the owner, who confirmed that she wasn't the first person to say they have seen this apparition.

The owner then told the waitress the story of when she bought the restaurant three years ago. One night, it was just she, her son, and his friend in the restaurant. Her son's friend stepped outside to smoke a cigarette. While smoking, he looked up and saw a man in the window staring down at him. The man had an angry and scowling visage. The young man went back into the restaurant and asked her: "What is the deal with that guy upstairs? Is he racist or something? Does he not like Spanish people?" She assured the young man that there was no one upstairs. In fact, the area in which the young man saw the nasty man peering out the window at him is part of the attic—the unfinished attic. One has to walk along the beams as there is no floor in this attic.

The waitress went on to say that before being gutted, this area of the attic housed several rooms for boarders. One night while driving by with her sister around 11:00 p.m., she clearly saw a lamp lit through one of the windows of the attic. She noticed this lamp several times while driving by late at night. Once she started working at the pub, she asked the owner: "Why do you leave that lamp on in the attic some nights?" The owner replied: "What lamp? There's no electricity up there. Maybe you saw the reflection of one of the parking lot lights in the window?" The waitress maintains the light was incandescent— unlike the blue light of the parking lot lights.

The basement is a key area for haunted activity. One day, the waitress went to the storeroom in the basement to retrieve some items. She didn't bother to turn the light on for the other end of the hallway where the restrooms are located. As she was making her way to the stairs from the storeroom with her hands full, she heard a female voice emanate from the darkened hallway. It simply said: "Hello?" The waitress said "hello" in return and ran up the stairs. After telling her sister what happened, her sister told her: "That was stupid! You never respond to ghosts!"

Author's interjection: At this point, let me clarify the sister's admonition, as best I can. When I was seventeen years old, I had a part-time job as a dietary aide working in the basement kitchen of a nursing home. One night, one of the nurses came into the kitchen and said: "Laura!" I was busy at the sink prepping dishes in the dish rack for the dishwasher. So, without turning around, I answered: "Yes. Can I help you?" Well, next thing I knew, this nurse grabbed my arm and forced me to turn and face her. She then said: "Child! Don't you know better than to answer without looking to see who's talking to you?" I was confused and scared, and simply said: "No. I'm sorry." She released my arm and instructed me to follow her to the employee dining room as the kitchen was too noisy. Once in the dining room, she asked me: "Do you know about the veil? Being born with a veil?" I said: "No." She explained to me that she was born with a veil, which is a thin piece of skin attached at the top of the forehead and it extends over the face. It was surgically removed, but it leaves its psychic mark on the individual. She told me of her gift of "second sight" and various lessons from the "PTB" (Powers That Be) she had accrued over the years.

The nurse told me to never answer to my name being called without first making sure there is someone corporeal present who called to me. She said: "The Devil plays tricks, child, and he can mimic your parents' voices, your friends, your teachers voices. If you answer the Devil, you've invited him in. You understand me?

62

It's possession, child; be very careful!" To this day, I always turn around and look to make sure someone is there before I respond to my name being called.

The waitress went on to say that since that "hello" in the basement and her response to it, she's been a primary witness, and sometimes target, of paranormal activity while at work. Juice boxes have fallen on her head while retrieving something from a lower shelf in the refrigerator. Since she's particular about the way she stocks the refrigerator and there is a "lip" at the end of each shelf to stop items from falling off the shelf, it can only point to an unseen hand knocking these juice boxes off the shelf and onto her head.

The ladies' room in the basement is also a focal point for ghostly encounters among patrons and employees. "In the year and a half that I have worked here, I've used that ladies' room twice," the waitress clarified. She refuses to go in there after dark. In fact, one night she and her sister were closing up and she was about to double check that she'd extinguished the candle in the ladies' room, but as she approached the room, she was overcome with a feeling of dread and goosebumps appeared on her arms. She couldn't go back in there. She reconciled that she must have blown out the candle previously since it was so dark down there. She and her sister ran back up the stairs and locked up for the night.

On one occasion, a customer was in the basement ladies' room, and while washing her hands, she looked into the mirror and saw a woman standing in back of her. When she turned to face this woman, no one was there. Another waitress had a chilling encounter as well. She was in one of the bathroom stalls when someone knocked on the stall door. She called out: "Just a minute." The knock came again. Again, she responded: "In a minute." The third time the knock came, she looked under the stall door and didn't see any feet—no one was there.

The owners' daughter noticed two women racing up the stairs from the basement ladies' room one time. When she asked them: "Is everything all right ladies," they said: "Were you knocking on the wall? The ladies' room wall…was that you knocking on it?" She assured them that she had been upstairs and would have no reason to knock on the wall.

The pool table exhibited paranormal activity when its side panel opened and crashed to the floor. The waitress explained that it was after closing and a few of the employees were gathered at the far end of the bar enjoying a drink and chatting when all of a sudden they heard a crash. The waitress showed me the panel on the side of the pool table. It has two locks, one on either end. One has to hold the panel in place while locking the first lock. No one was near the pool table when this panel came loose and fell to the floor. There was no huge vibration in the area to cause both locks to unlock and release the panel.

It is rumored that a former owner/bartender actually died behind the bar. He opened the bar one afternoon, as usual, and when patrons began arriving, he was nowhere in sight. They assumed he was in the kitchen, and waited patiently for him to return. Eventually, they began to search for him and found him dead behind the bar. It was determined he died from a heart attack. To this day, the owners and bartenders often wonder if it is "Gus" who turns the jukebox on and off late at night when the pub is quiet. "Gus" also enjoys knocking over tray stands at either end of the room. According to the owner: "The crashing sound of when they hit the hardwood floor is enough to make you jump out of your skin!"

Longtime patrons of the pub have told the owners of another death on the property involving a "regular" of the bar. He stumbled his way out the door after having consumed a large amount of alcohol. Instead of stumbling around the adjacent pond, he fell right into it and drowned. The following morning his body was found floating there. According to the owners, he was a distant relative of theirs and of the family branch that was one of the earliest settlers in the area.

Two different employees have encountered the ghost of a child on the stairs leading to the basement. The first employee was on his way to the basement with an armful of items for the storage room. When he got to the bottom of the stairs, he saw the child playing on the stairs in back of him via the mirror that used to hang on the wall facing the stairs. He turned around quickly and no one was there. Since then, the waitress said you can hear this employee skip steps and practically jump his way down the stairs to ensure his speed in getting to the storage room and getting back upstairs as quickly as possible.

The chef experienced the voice of a child calling "Mom, Mommy" when she came in early to do some baking. She swore it was her son even though she knew she did not bring him with her. The voice was so clear that it forced her to override her logic and go look for him anyway. Jen, the bartender, had a similar experience wherein she heard what she thought was her daughter's voice calling for her.

The bartender's son had a frightening experience on Mother's Day. He is a fourteen-year-old who absolutely loves horror movies and scary stuff. So, they didn't think anything of sending him down to the basement to retrieve some items from the coolers. He flew up the stairs in a state of panic. When they questioned him, he said that he heard the ghost talking in his ear. He couldn't understand what it was saying, but it definitely was that close to him and talking into his ear. Intuitively, the waitress picked flowers that were outside and went to the basement and offered them as a Mother's Day gift to the "mom ghost" and asked her not to scare the bartender's son like that again.

However, sometimes the ghost or ghosts have proven to be helpful. The bartender was struggling to get a glass into the hanging glass rack. She was on the tips of her toes, but just couldn't reach the rack in order to slide the glass in. Suddenly, she felt the glass lift from her hand and slide into the rack. Was this the ghost of the bartender helping her out?

The same bartender swears she saw a man sitting at one of the tables in the bar one night around midnight as she was driving by the pub. She knew her boss was going to close that night and couldn't understand why he would still be there—just sitting there. She called him and asked him what he was still doing at the pub. He said: "I'm home in bed. I closed up over an hour ago."

The waitress usually opens the pub on Sunday mornings. She said she comes in around 10:30 a.m. or so and begins to sweep the floors and set up for the day's business. As she was sweeping, the pub's phone rang. She answered it, and the owner was on the line. They exchanged greetings and then the owner asked: "So, what's up? Why did you call me?" The waitress said: "I didn't call you. You called me. I was busy sweeping." Later that day, the owner showed the missed call from Tom X Pub entry on her cellphone's index to the waitress.

Unfortunately, I didn't have the best conditions to investigate the Tom X Pub as it was in full swing for dinner when I was there. The EVP session I attempted in the basement ladies' room was fraught with background noise from the vent and fan as well as the restaurant above me. However, on a subsequent visit with my husband, we had better luck during our EVP sessions. Kent was able to capture what sounds like a woman's voice saying: "I'm here." I was able to record a knocking response to my query: "If there's somebody here, can you knock on the door?" However, the knocking sound did not seem to come from the door to the restroom, rather it emanated from within the restroom. Later, during this EVP session, I asked: "Can you tell me your name? Are you lost?" Six faint, quick knocks are heard in response. I thought I heard a woman's voice whispering, but after careful examination of the recording, I realized that the sound was water trickling down the pipes, probably from someone running water via one of the sinks upstairs.

As for the Tom X Pub being haunted, I would say "yes." The basement ladies' room is definitely harboring some discarnate soul. I could sense it, her. It's simple: X marks the spot for a potential full-body apparition or Class A EVP, as well as a great cheeseburger.

CHAPTER 11

Hotel Fauchère

A fine place to stay, dine, and see the ghostly little boy.

Born in Switzerland in 1823, Fauchère came to the United States with his wife and daughter in 1851. He secured work as a master chef at the Delmonico Restaurant in New York City, famed restaurant and birthplace of the namesake Delmonico steak. By 1867, Fauchère purchased property in Milford, Pennsylvania; it was a little saloon named "Van Gorden & LaBar." As word spread of his cuisine, his business grew. Later, he moved the saloon to the rear of the property and continued his business while the new, larger hotel of his dreams was being constructed. The Italianate structure, with its twenty-four guest rooms and dining room, was opened for business in 1880.

In addition to the hotel, he acquired a little brick cottage on Catherine Street. His former employer, the Delmonicos, stayed there so frequently, that it became known as the Delmonico Cottage.

After Louis Fauchère died in 1893, his daughter, Marie Fauchère Chol Tissot, took over the business. The hotel and restaurant remained in the family's operation until 1976 when the property was sold.

The building was used as a medical practice facility and eventually fell into disrepair. It sat abandoned for ten years until the current owner, Sean Strub, purchased it. He invested heavily in the building's restoration to return it to a hotel and restaurant in all its glory.

The minute one enters the hotel, the gorgeous white with black diamond accent marble-tiled floor catches the eye. This flooring is original. The Delmonico fine dining restaurant is open for intimate, romantic dinners on the weekends and breakfast throughout the week with brunch on Sundays. The Bar Louis in the lower level provides a relaxed atmosphere as well as lunches and dinners that delight the palate. This bar was created along with its outside access door under the management of Warren Chol, Louis Fauchère's grandson.

In 1906, the hotel purchased the house to the left of it that was built by Dr. Emerson. The doctor's wife died soon after the construction of the house; therefore, Dr. Emerson was too grief stricken to reside there. Originally, the house was used to accommodate overflow guests of the hotel. Today, it is home to their Pâtisserie Fauchère, which makes the most amazing brioche, eclairs, artisan breads, and canine cookies. Freyja and Uri, our Rottweilers, gave two paws up for these dog biscuits.

Guest rooms range from superior to deluxe to premium and all include Internet access, heated towel racks, and radiant heated bathroom floors. Continental breakfast and off-street parking add to the convenience factor that rounds out a stay here perfectly.

Pâtisserie Fauchère—ghostly shadows appear in the dining room.

If you have a significant other who has zero interest in ghost hunting or the paranormal, but enjoys a pampered get-away, Hotel Fauchère will make you both exceedingly happy. I met with Nicki, bartender/wait staff of the hotel for the past two years, who shared with me her ghostly encounter. Over the summer, she would be one of the first people to arrive for work in the morning, usually around 6:45 a.m. As she entered the Delmonico dining room, there would be a little boy standing near and facing the grand piano. He was dressed in clothing similar to the late 1800s or early 1900s. He would never turn to face her. In fact, he didn't move at all. His head was facing down towards the floor, but his back was always to Nicki and his face towards the piano. She said the first time she saw him, she was caught her off guard and the apparition startled her. Nicki said if she looked directly at him, he would vanish within seconds of staring at him. However, if she went about her business—seemingly ignoring him—he would remain standing there longer and slowly fade from view each time she entered the room. Nicky thinks this ghost may be the spirit of the boy whose picture hangs in the restaurant—Warren Chol, Louis Fauchère's grandson.

The ghost boy stares at this grand piano and then vanishes from view.

The ghost boy who appears at the piano may be Warren Chol, Louis Fauchère's grandson.

Nicky told me about the time her manager and a co-worker were talking while standing at the servers' station. All of the sudden, they stopped talking and began to shiver. Then they said aloud how freezing cold they were, and that they figured it was the ghost going right by them. Nicky said: "I was standing near them, and I didn't feel anything."

A few years ago, a busboy/dishwasher was working very late—around 1:00 or 2:00 a.m. He heard a little boy call for his mother. The busboy stopped washing dishes and went to check to see if a little boy was wandering in the hallways. He did not find the boy. No one was around. So, he went back to washing dishes. A few minutes later, he heard the boy calling for his mom again, only this time it sounded like the boy was right in back of him. He turned around to see no one there. He gave up doing the dishes and left immediately.

The sudden drop in temperature and the discarnate voice are indicative of an active haunting. Yet, the apparition of the boy staring at the piano is more of a residual haunt. For some reason, emotional or habitual, the essence of little Warren is locked in a type of loop tape that plays itself sporadically.

According to Tim, the town's ghost walk tour guide: "The Fauchère is said to have a residual haunting of Rudolph Valentino. He is seen gazing out of a corner window." At the time of his actual stay at the hotel, the young ladies gathered on Catherine Street in the hopes of seeing him through that window. Their excitement and euphoria left a thumb print in time that manifests as seeing Valentino in that same window to this day.

I met with Carly at the Pâtisserie. She has worked there for a little over a year. She told me about the time she was closing up for the day and saw a shadow glide across the floor of the bakery. Given the way the sun was coming in the windows at that time of day, she figured someone must have still been in the dining area. She walked over to the dining area and found no one there. She told me: "Even if a car had gone by, which it hadn't, but if it had, it would have made a blinding reflection—not black shadow."

It is said that after Louis Fauchère died, his wife asked that his signature dish "Chicken Margengo" never be made again at the restaurant. She was convinced that no one ever would make it the way he did. Perhaps she should have added to that request that the only spirits allowed in the place were the ones on the shelf in Bar Louis.

70

Memorytown

The Print Shop Ghost and the Blue Lady lend a hand in making memories.

Poconos

This quaint attraction nestled on 200 bucolic acres in the heart of Mount Pocono on Grange Road is reminiscent of days gone by. I have fond memories of this place from my childhood. From the confectionery shop, which used to sell the best homemade fudge along with other tooth-decaying delights, to the candle and soap shops, Memorytown is an appropriate moniker. The memories have been created for the next generation via my sons who had their first paddle boat ride here.

Today, Memorytown is creating stunning memories for brides who choose this venue for their weddings. The barn has been renovated to create lavish receptions while maintaining an earthy, down-home appeal. The website for Memorytown is comprehensive and attractive. From rodeos to horseback riding to ATV rides, there is something to entertain everyone.

Its history starts with the Wagner family who settled this area in 1852, after squatting on the 400-acre property since 1826. George E. Wagner, born in 1868, was the founder of the Christmas tree nursery business. By 1947, Memorytown was in business for the burgeoning tourism industry of the Poconos.

Are there ghosts here? Yes and no. Not every bump in the night or eerie wailing sound is the result of a discarnate being. A ghost hunter has to be a skeptic and pragmatic in their approach to a reportedly haunted location. I spoke with owner, Anthony Maula, about his experiences with "the other side" at Memorytown. He told me about the time his father, brother, and he were in the building that houses the old Print Shop. They all heard this banging sound: *bang, bang, bang*. It was followed by a forlorn and chilling wail. They stopped what they were doing and saying and listened. It came again. *Bang, bang, bang!* And the wailing sound followed suit. Anthony began to move toward the source of the sounds. He determined they were emanating from the Print Shop. As he was picking up speed in his pace, he said to his brother and father: "It's coming from the Print Shop. You hear it too, right?" He took a few more steps and realized no response came from his brother or father. Anthony turned around and realized they had bolted out the first available exit.

Resolved to figure out what was making this banging and wailing sound, Anthony continued on. When he arrived at the Print Shop, he found a drunken man banging a stick on the door that he was propped up against. The wailing sound was this gentleman calling for help—or another round perhaps? Either way, the frightening event came to a non-paranormal end.

Memories made for the author's sons, Brian and Trent, at Memorytown. Inset photo is at ages five and eleven and background is at ages eighteen and twenty-four.

Yet, there was the time when Ted and Kim of Markou Paranormal Investigations visited Memorytown. Anthony toured them through the various buildings. They employed video cameras and other ghost-hunting gadgets. In the Print Shop, he paused for a moment and said to them: "It's like no one ever left here." Upon data review, the team discovered an EVP immediately following Anthony's quote. The whispered voice said: "Big shot." When the team played this EVP for Anthony, he laughed thinking: "Great. So the ghost is insulting me, how nice."

About two to three weeks later, Anthony was working at his computer trying to come up with a font for use on the website and in print media. He had some old advertising literature as guides. Finally, he found a font that not only captured the nostalgic essence of Memorytown, but it matched perfectly to what had been used in previous advertising pieces. The name of the font is "Big shot." It stands to reason that the Print Shop ghost was offering professional advice, not an insult.

As for a visual encounter of the Print Shop ghost, according to Charles J. Adams III, author of *Pocono Ghosts, Legends and Lore, Book Two*, a former employee saw this ghost by the Print Shop door. The former employee said: "He just appeared and disappeared." It is suspected that this is the ghost of a former resident who lived near the pond. The rumors of this man's death include committing suicide to being killed while feeding his farm animals.

The most famous ghost of Memorytown is the Blue Lady. She is described as being in her twenties, having long, dark hair and wearing a long, blue dress. Her ghostly resume includes flicking lights on and off, opening doors, changing the radio station to her preferred gospel music, and hearing her footsteps make their way across the floor. Sightings of the Blue Lady have dwindled severely in recent times.

However, another ghostly sound has been added to the repertoire. Anthony told me about his electrician/friend. This man is a former Navy Seal—a real "bad ass," but in a good military way. While this man was doing some electrical work at Memorytown, he heard children laughing and running back and forth on the floor above him. He knew he was the only one in the building at that time. This event rattled the former Seal to his core.

The spirits of Memorytown are harmless, and in Anthony's experience, actually helpful. Whether you're in the Poconos for a day trip or a long weekend, Memorytown should be on your short list of places to visit.

CHAPTER 13

The Columns Museum

Madame Peirce's artifacts are on the second floor, along with her ghostly presence.

In 1796, the village of Milford was designed by John Biddis, inventor of white lead paint and recipient of one of the first US Patent Office's patents issued for his tar that was used in tanning. By Christmas 1874, the town was incorporated, and today is the county seat for Pike County. The town is picturesque with its Victorian homes and buildings.

A stand-out building is the neoclassical designed Columns Museum, which is home to the Pike County Historical Society (PCHS). Lori Strelecki, director for the past fifteen years, was kind enough to meet with me to discuss the history and the haunting of the Columns.

The historical society's prized possession is the Lincoln Flag, which was recently returned to them after being on display for two months at Ford's Theater, in Washington, DC, for the 150th Anniversary of Lincoln's assassination.

Ms. Strelecki explained how the flag came to Milford initially. In 1865, Thomas Gourlay was the stage manager at Ford's Theater, and his daughter, Jeannie Gourlay, was performing in the production *Our American Cousin*. After President Lincoln was shot in the back of the head, this flag that was draped from the front of his theater box was used as a make-shift pillow for his head. After Lincoln was carried across the street to the Petersen house, where he later died, Mr. Gourlay kept the flag. He gave it to his daughter, Jeannie, before he died. She left it to her son, V. Paul Struthers, and, in 1954, he donated it, along with some of his mother's stage costumes, hats, and shoes, to the PCHS.

The Columns mansion was built in 1904 for Dennis McLaughlin, a wealthy businessman from Hoboken, New Jersey. Upon his doctor's suggestion to have a little country home to escape to every so often, this twenty-two room mansion became McLaughlin's summer home. He sold the mansion in 1930, and it changed hands several times thereafter and endured different incarnations, such as a dance studio, bar, restaurant, boarding house, and VFW headquarters. By 1980, the PCHS bought the run-down mansion and restored it beautifully. PCHS finally had a place to call "home," having operated since 1930 without a headquarters.

Although Ms. Strelecki has never personally experienced any haunting or ghosts in the mansion, she believes others have. She said, to date, between eight and nine people have relayed similar experiences to her independent of each other.

People have reported hearing the rustling of taffeta and sensing the presence of a female spirit in the Peirce room. Reports are consistent in that this female spirit never leaves

The flag stained with President Lincoln's blood when it was used to cushion his head after being shot at Ford's Theatre.

the second floor and is primarily in the Peirce room or wandering the hallways. Docents working at the Columns agree there is a dense atmosphere of Madame Peirce's room. Sally H., a docent for several years, senses a female ghost.

Perhaps this is the spirit of Juliette Annette Froissy, the widow of Charles Sanders Peirce, scholar and founder of "pragmatism." Charles and Juliette never resided in the Columns, but did live in Milford. The Peirce room houses some of their belongings, from Charles' hat box to Juliette's mourning clothes.

A former teacher at the University of Scranton came to visit the Columns. After touring the museum, she approached Ms. Strelecki's office and stood in the doorway with a troubled expression on her face. Ms. Strelecki asked: "What's wrong?" The woman sat down and explained her capability of getting visions. She went on to tell each one of these visions she experienced during her self-guided tour.

In the front room, the Lincoln room, she got the vision of people dancing. Interesting since at one time this building was a dance studio and that is the room in which the classes were held. Downstairs she got the image of a child—well the body and height of a child, but an old woman's face. Ms. Strelecki explained that one of the interns used to bring her younger sister with her on occasion. This little girl had progeria—a medical condition in which the body ages well beyond the chronological age of the individual. This little girl loved to play "talk show" in the basement conference room.

The woman continued with having had a flash of someone being pushed down the third-floor servant stairs. She sensed that it was an accident resulting from an argument. This may have been related to the time Mr. McLaughlin was amorously pursuing the nanny after the death of his second wife. By some accounts, the nanny refused his proposal of marriage.

Ms. Strelecki's only experience with something odd at the museum was during one of the sleepovers that the scouts had. She tried to sleep in the basement with them, but the kids like to be up until the wee hours talking and laughing. She then attempted to sleep on the floor of her office, but she could still hear them. Finally, she went up to the second floor and crawled into a bed that was there at that time. It wasn't a piece of furniture with historical value, and, therefore, she didn't see the harm in trying to get somewhat of a good night's sleep. Her dog Lucky refused to lay down in the room with her. This was a dog that was always glued to her side, yet this time, the dog refused. The next morning she found the dog asleep downstairs in her office.

After my interview with Ms. Strelecki, I took time to tour the mansion. I was allowed to take pictures, without the flash of course. I put my digital audio recorder on in case any errant spirits wanted to leave a message.

In speaking with Linda Zimmermann, author of the *Ghost Investigator* series of books, she told me the following of her experience at the Columns: "No EVPs or photos I can recall, but for me it was even better, and much more personal. As I was looking at that bizarre hair-curling chair/device, I felt a finger go up under my hat and move back and forth. I felt a very strong female presence, and knew she had just read me like a book and knew who I was. Later, I heard the swishing of long skirts on the first floor and ran after the sound, 100% certain she wanted me to find something. The sounds led me to the back office, where there is a bank of big file cabinets. I opened a drawer and pulled out a file, not having a clue what I was looking for, and came upon an article about me and my ghost hunting! I believe it was Juliette Peirce, and she wanted me to know that she knew who I was to validate that she was there. This still remains perhaps the most amazing thing that ever happened to me on an investigation."

History buffs Laura Badea, of Badea and Soul Day Spa, and her husband visited the Columns when they were looking to move to Milford seven years ago. While she was upstairs in the hallway outside the bathroom that connects the two bedrooms, she saw a mannequin in the back bedroom out of the corner of her eye. "It was like she was alive. I mean, I know she wasn't. It was just a mannequin; she didn't walk or talk. But I had more of a feeling. There was an overwhelming energy from that back room. It really was Madame Peirce's energy. It was so strong that I couldn't go back there." When she was filmed for the show Ghost Detectives, Laura discovered other people had the same experience as she had.

As for the basement, Laura said she used to attend card games there. "There is the one corner that I would avoid. I didn't even want to look in that direction because I just knew something was there." She went on to say that she sensed the presence of a small person there. It was hard for her to describe because she said it resembled an old person's face, but the stature of a child. I told her she was probably sensing the child who had progeria who used to play in the basement.

Tim Kelly is the tour guide for the local ghost walk tours of Milford. While he did not have any personal ghostly encounters to relay about the Columns, he did have some interesting ghost stories about growing up just six miles away from the mansion.

As for a team that investigated the Columns and came up with some EVPs, I spoke with Barbara of Sullivan Paranormal. They have been investigating for over two years and are developing a respectable reputation in their area as well as the Milford area. Her team investigated in August 2015, and using the "ghost box" got some specific answers to their questions. They were holding this session in Madame Peirce's room on the second floor. Barbara asked: "Is Juliette here?" The response came clearly in a woman's voice saying: "Yes, I am." Other voices were recorded including a male and a child's voice. When the team asked: "How many are here?" The answer came in a little girl's voice as: "Six." There were six team members present that night. Another EVP captured was that of an adult female voice that said: "I'm lost." Given the team achieved approximately fourteen direct responses during this session, they have committed to returning with another set of direct and succinct questions for the spirits of the Columns. Their goal is to procure answers that would be substantiated historically.

Interview with Tim Kelly

Tour Guide for Local Ghost Walking Tours

The house he grew up in was on the old Milford-Owego Turnpike. Prior to being his single-family home, it was a stagecoach stop and a bakery. The house itself always had a lot of electrical problems, such as lights and the televisions going and on and off by themselves. One particular event that stands out for him was when he and his girlfriend were on the couch watching television. The answering machine, which at that time used analog cassette tapes to record messages, started to make weird clicking noises, like someone was tapping on it. His girlfriend looked at him as if to say: "Why is it doing that?" Tim, who by this point was used to the odd sounds of the house, just shrugged it off and continued to watch the television. The answering machine started to make more noises. This time it was the sound of a dial tone and then the tones of numbers being pressed as if someone was dialing a phone number. Next, they heard the ringing of the placed call playing over the speaker of the answering machine. Then, Tim recognized his grandfather's voice saying: "Hello? Hello?" Tim jumped off the couch and picked up the receiver of the phone and said: "Hello, Gramps. How are you?" His grandfather asked him what he wanted, and Tim was perplexed and said: "Mom and Dad aren't home now. Did you need something?" His grandfather said: "You called me." Tim was still confused but did not want to argue with his grandfather, so he continued the conversation until its natural close.

In retrospect, Tim feels that it was his grandmother, who had passed away several years prior, who initiated that phone call between Tim and his grandfather. She must have sensed how sad and lonely her husband was and made a "special trip" to intervene on his behalf.

Tim's mother witnessed a Crisis Apparition of his Grandmother. (To clarify, a Crisis Apparition occurs usually at the time of death or shortly thereafter. The spirit of the newly deceased makes the rounds to loved ones in an effort to say "good-bye.") His mom was on the second floor and heard someone coming up the stairs. She went to see who it was, and it was her mother. She watched as the apparition arrived at the second floor, turned, and went into the bedroom where Tim and his siblings were asleep. His mother went to the doorway of this bedroom and saw the ghost of her mother looking over the bed at the sleeping children. The grandmother ghost then turned around to face his mother and dissolved from view.

Another time, their neighbor, who was taking care of their cat while they were away, drove by the house on her way home. She noticed all the lights were on. Not sure why they would come home early and not tell her, she immediately turned the car around and went back to confirm they were home. As she approached the house, just minutes later, it was completely dark.

Having grown up in a haunted house, Tim makes the quintessential ghost tour guide. I recommend visiting the Columns and taking his tour when in Milford. Neither will disappoint.

e Poconos

CHAPTER 14

The Covered Bridge Inn

*Cold brews and eerie shadows
are on tap.*

The Covered Bridge Inn in Palmerton is a quaint bar and restaurant. The building dates back to the 1800s and was a key stop on the stagecoach route to Philadelphia. Across the street is the restaurant's namesake, the covered bridge.

I have been to this restaurant several times since moving to this area. Of course, I had to ask: "Is this place haunted?" The waitress was all too pleased to reply: "Yes!" She even pointed out the owner's wife to me who was seated at the bar. I approached Carol and introduced myself. She confirmed that in the years she and her husband have owned the place a few strange things have happened. She clarified with: "Nothing terrifying or evil—just strange."

She told me about the cook who used to board in one of the rooms upstairs, and that he would swear he heard someone walking around downstairs in the bar when he knew it was not open for business. A couple of times, he went down to see if it was one of the owners arriving early to drop off some goods, but he would discover that he was, in fact, the only one in the building.

Carol went on to say how little things would go missing. Bartenders typically experienced these phenomena. They would be prepping limes for bar drinks, put the knife down to answer a phone call or greet a customer at the bar, and when they would turn their attention back to the limes, the knife would be missing. After interrogating everyone else who had access to the bar, they would find it in the prep sink or on another counter.

On our most recent visit to the Covered Bridge Inn, Kent and I decided to sit and eat at the bar. It was unusually quiet for a Friday night. After we finished eating, I asked Amanda, the bartender, if she had had any paranormal experiences while working. She said in the seven and a half years she's worked there, not really. Well, except for the one time the bar trays crashed to the floor. She didn't see it happen, but heard the crash and saw the wooden trays on the floor behind the bar. She cannot explain how they fell since they were stored properly. Other than that, she has only experienced this feeling of a "presence" being in the bar standing over by the entrance to the ladies' rest room. Amanda has no idea who this presence may be, but she has the sense of it being "male." She said sometimes she senses him being there and staring at her. Sometimes this feeling is intense; she will turn around quickly to try to see him there. But, when she does, no one is there.

The restaurant's namesake—the covered bridge.

We did notice a foul odor on this last visit. It would have made for a great story to say that it was the funk of a demon, but that is not the case. Apparently, there were some septic issues going on, and that was the source for the odor.

This is not a highly active place for the paranormal, but it does deserve an "honorable mention."

CHAPTER 15

The Lake House Hotel

A haunted house attraction that's actually haunted.

e Pocono

The Lake House Hotel started out as a stagecoach stop in the late 1700s. Tavern construction began in 1820 and opened in 1847 under the management and ownership of Charles Saylor. Perched on the corner of Old Route 115/Wilkes-Barre Turnpike and Cherry Valley Road, it provided guests from New York City and Philadelphia the peace and quiet of a mountain resort in the Poconos with accessibility to Saylors Lake. It served as a post office and tavern. After a fire, it was rebuilt and renamed the Lake House Hotel.

My mother remembers visiting during family vacations as a girl. She said it was the place to go to for the dance parties. Beautiful colored lights illuminated the footpath to the large dock by the lake. There was a stage for the band and a bar and grill for refreshments. She was never a guest of the Lake House Hotel as my grandparents either booked a cabin on the Possinger farm or another local cabin-based lodging in Reeders.

By the 1970s, the Lake House was in its "faded glory" stage and was merely a bar and venue for bar fights. After it closed, it sat abandoned for nearly twenty years. Eventually, it was opened as a haunted house attraction. However, in 2010, the Lake House was purchased by Marlo and Dan Ambrosio. They maintained it as a haunted house attraction but revamped it to theater-level fright and dubbed it "The Hotel of Horror."

I met "Dead Dan" at the ParaFest convention, September 2013, in Bethlehem, Pennsylvania. He was the curator of the Exhibition Macabre, a "museum" housed in the basement of the hotel. Its static displays include bizarre medical experiments and mortuary details of preparation of the dead. Dead Dan invited me to stop in to see the display and also to "take some readings" with my ghost-hunting gear as he was convinced there was something otherworldly residing there. By the time I got a chance to follow up with Dead Dan, after the Halloween season, it was too late. I sent him an email and got a response from the owner, Marlo, stating that the place was closed for the season and no access could be granted.

Fortunately for me, many paranormal groups have visited the Lake House over the years. Bob Christopher's group, N.E.P.A. Paranormal, has investigated the place and shared their findings via video posts on YouTube©.

As for seeing the Lake House/Horror Hotel on the big screen, in 2012 a movie titled *6 Degrees of Hell*, starring Corey Feldman, was filmed here. Subsequent to its red carpet premier at the Sherman Theater in Stroudsburg, the movie retained a faint pulse of recognition in the occult-horror films section thanks to Feldman's *Lost Boys* fame."

good Evening and Welcome
to the Lake House Hotel,
Tavern and Restaurant.

Please begin with one
of our
Exciting Introductions...

Clams Casino $2.⁷⁵   French Onion Soup $1.⁵⁰
Shrimp Cocktail $3.⁵⁰   gratinée
Soup 'Du Jour $1.²⁵   Sautéed Mushrooms $1.⁵⁰
Garlic Bread $1.⁰⁰   Stuffed Mushrooms $2.²⁵
                                  marinara

Old menu from the Lake House Hotel.

Poconos

According to fellow author Kenneth Biddle, who wrote *Haunted Lehigh Valley*, the haunting of the Lake House includes the spirits of the former bartender, a miner, and possibly a suicide victim. According to authors, Charles J. Adams III and Dennis William Hauck, "Suicide Ridge" is off Bonser Road in Saylorsburg, Ross Township. This ridge supposedly saw several suicides beginning in the 1930s with the Werkheiser father and son suicide. After extensive research, I cannot validate these suicides at all. Werkheiser is a big family name in this area and their farm is still in operation. I followed up with a lead I derived from Mr. Adams' book only to be told that the information given to him was created simply to amuse the gentleman butcher and his son. I have traveled up and down the roads cited for these suicides at various times of day and night, and not once encountered any earth-bound spirits.

As for the ghost of the bartender, his story is that he was severely beaten in an attempted robbery and died a few days later of complications from his injuries. Given the history of the bar falling into a "fight club" setting, this has a glimmer of potentiality, but again, I cannot find any news articles to substantiate it. However, I interviewed "Kim" who worked at the haunted house attraction for five years. She knew nothing of this bartender-robbery story. She told me that in 2012, she saw her first ever full-body apparition.

She was one of the four actors staged in the "Demonic Church" in the attic. She was in position on the stage kneeling under the light that was timed to turn on and off every few seconds. One of the other actors was on the side of the stage positioned at the microphone that was equipped with a mechanism to change one's voice to something demonically unrecognizable. The other two actors were out in the pew section. There was a lull between tours coming through. Kim took advantage of this lull to check her cellphone. While checking the phone for texts and missed calls, she "heard" something in her head telling her to "turn around." It was so clear and strong that she stood up and turned around and was face-to-ghostly-face with the apparition of a tall, thin man. He was not translucent. He was as solid as anyone could be. He appeared to be beat up and his white dress shirt was tattered. He had on black pants that were ratty at the cuffs, and dress shoes. Kim said that he did not appear to be from "the olden days," but more likely from the 1970s or 1980s. He had dark brown hair that was shaggy, there was dirt on his face, and he stood somewhat slumped over.

She said: "He looked like he was just miserable." Strangely enough, Kim was not overcome with fear. She stood there staring him in the face and "heard" various things in her head such as "bartender," "waiter," and the name "William." She was feeling his feelings of sadness, anger, and confusion. With that, the timed light turned off and when it turned back on, the apparition was gone. I asked her how old she thought he was and she said he appeared to be in his early thirties or late twenties. Kim never saw him again, even though she wished she had as she wanted to know more about him. She asked other actors if they ever saw him, and no one had. The closest she got was a security guard friend of hers who said he had seen the shadow of a man in a white shirt running through the halls on different occasions. Each time, he thought it was one of the patrons, but then he would realize the next tour hadn't actually come through yet.

The death of the miner is not documented in news articles, but has a faint capacity for truth because of the Blue Ridge Enameled Brick Company. The company was founded as Penn Buff Brick in 1894 and changed its name in 1901. Given the superior clay in the Saylorsburg area, the company produced a white, shiny glazed enamel brick. The plant was based on 240 acres in the Hamilton and Ross Township area. Mining the prized clay involved using two shafts measuring six feet wide and 150 feet deep. One shaft provided air for the miners and the other one allowed for transportation of the miners and their equipment.

A fatally wounded miner being carried to the front porch of the Lake House Hotel is plausible given the nearest hospital at that time would have been close to a four-hour ride by horse-drawn vehicle.

And finally, the purported suicide relates that a gentleman checked into the Lake House Hotel, went to his room on the second floor, and hanged himself. Typically with suicides, obituaries do not recount the death as suicide in deference to the surviving family members. The only proof of a Saylorsburg suicide I was able to find was the front page article in the *Morning Press* newspaper, dated November 2, 1914. It details that Mr. Harry Miller was distraught over his inability to pay his boarding debt to Mr. Robert Smale, proprietor of the Poponoming Inn. Miller hanged himself from an apple tree close to the inn's location.

So, is the Lake House actually haunted? Yes. I say this based on the experiences of the various actors of the haunted house attraction. Several actors have seen the security guard at a certain spot in the haunted house and then minutes later see him in a totally different location in the attraction. When they questioned the guard: "how did you get from there to here so fast," he confirmed that he was not in the first location they saw him. Other reports include being pushed and touched by unseen hands. "Kevin," a veteran actor, saw a shadow of a person enter his room and proceed down the long hallway. "Kevin" used a shortcut in the hopes of confronting this person in the adjacent hallway. However, he found no one there. Further, there wasn't any other way for that person to exit the building.

I interviewed Joey S., another veteran actor of the Hotel of Horror. He performed at the haunted house in 2013. The funeral room was his performance room, and it was in the back portion of the building's attic. While in that room he would hear footsteps walking near him and across the room, yet no corporeal being besides him was in the room at that time. He would feel someone lightly touching the small of his back, and, again, no one was there. When he went to get a bottle of water from a nearby room, he heard the footsteps charge in the opposite direction of where he was heading. Joey said there was enough residual light that he would have been able to see someone moving in that direction, but he didn't see anyone. He thought maybe the footsteps were the result of the floorboards vibrating from the motion sensitive air compressor in the other room, but there was no one in that room at that time to trigger the air compressor to discharge.

One night, he was sitting in his room and he sensed that someone was in there with him. He mentally said: "Good, you're here. Help me scare these patrons that are about to come through here." Shortly afterwards, a group of four girls entered his room. He kept his head down and facing the floor. He slowly lifted his head and began to stand up. Just then, the last girl entering the room through the curtains screamed bloody murder. She said: "Someone just grabbed my shoulder!" Joey was nowhere near her and as per protocol of the haunted house, the actors are not allowed to touch the patrons.

As a patron, Joey has experienced a genuine scare at the Hotel of Horror. He told me it was the first time they offered a "Lights Out" attraction. Patrons were given a small flashlight and allowed to meander through the hotel in complete darkness save for the dim light generated by the tiny flashlight.

90

Photo courtesy of Joey Scalzo as he performed as
"IronHeart" at the Hotel of Horror.

As he and his partner, Greg, were making their way through
the building, Joey sensed someone following uncomfortably
close behind him. It was so strong, that even though he
turned around and verified several times that no one was
physically there, he began pushing Greg along to get through
the hotel faster. Once outside, Greg said to him: "I know
what you were doing. You felt like someone was right behind
you, didn't you?"

While I can't confirm the identity of the spirits at the
Hotel of Horror, I can confirm they checked in and have yet
to check out.

CHAPTER 16

St. Mark's Church
Jim Thorpe

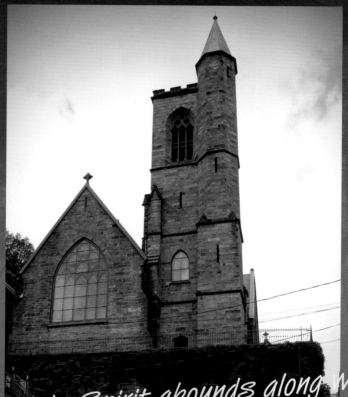

*The Holy Spirit abounds along with
the spirit of Mary Packer Cummings.*

The Episcopalian congregation of St. Mark's dates back to 1829. The present-day Gothic revival church designed by architect Richard Upjohn Sr. was ready for services in 1869.

Mary Packer Cummings was the main benefactor for St. Mark's. She funded the addition of the elevator to save people from having to walk up forty stairs. She insisted on being the first person to ride in the elevator once renovations were completed. Sadly, in 1912, she died a few days before they completed the installation of the Otis elevator. However, holding true to her request, Mary made the maiden voyage in her casket.

Mary was the daughter of Asa Packer, a wealthy man who founded the Lehigh Valley Railroad and Lehigh University. She willed her father's mansion to the town of Mauch Chunk as a tribute to her father. She also donated the Tiffany stained-glass window titled: "The Breadth of My Love" in memory of her sister, Lucy, to St. Mark's Church. Mary financed the construction of a small chapel for the cold winter months when attendance of weekly services was not as large. Rather than heat the huge church, it was more cost-effective to warm the small chapel and comfortably accommodate the smaller crowd.

I interviewed Carleen Ladden who operates and leads the ghost tours in Jim Thorpe. She has been conducting these tours for the past six years. She is an office worker, tour guide, paranormal investigator (of Paranormal Sightings of Pennsylvania investigative group) and choral singer with the Bach Handel Chorale. Her walking ghost tours start at the Inn at Jim Thorpe, continue up Broadway to the Old Jail, and then come back down Race Street to conclude at the train station. Her tour takes about an hour and a half and is one mile.

Some tours have the added benefit of an inexplicable occurrence or ghostly encounter. One time she was touring a group and noticed that at every spot she would stop the tour to do her presentation, the street light would go out. She later asked the other tour guides if that had happened to them, and they said: "No."

The fire house, which is attached to the opera house, is a hot spot for orb pictures taken of her during the tours. In 2014, while on the tour, she advised the group of this fact and stood there patiently while several pictures were taken of her. As the tour continued from this spot, a husband and wife remained behind so the husband could take pictures of

his wife standing where Carleen had just stood. The next thing Carleen knew, they were yelling: "Wait! Come back! Come back! Look at this!" Carleen returned to them, and they showed her the picture the husband had taken of his wife. There was the image of a woman all in black—like a silhouette—standing in back of the man's wife in the picture.

Another time, after a concert at the Opera House, Carleen did a private ghost walk for a group of approximately twenty-five to thirty people. It was an unusually large group. By the time they got to the steps of St. Mark's Church, it was around 12:30 a.m. Carleen stood on the steps with her back to the door giving her talk. Suddenly, it sounded like someone was standing on the other side of the church doors and took both their fists and slammed them against the door. The sound and vibration were so loud and intense that she shot forward into the group and stabilized herself by taking hold of a man's arm. The rest of the group backed up in fright. They all heard it. When she got home later, she told her boyfriend about the episode, and he dismissed it as rattling pipes and banging radiators resulting from their expansion when the heat came on. She made it a point to inspect this area of the church the next time she was there on the inside, and discovered there were no radiators or pipes to supply heat in that area.

In retrospect, Carleen thinks that the spirit of Mary Packer Cummings was probably unhappy with the tour being conducted that late at night on the church steps. While formal investigations are not allowed in the church or either of the Packer mansions, Carleen has captured suspicious orb photos when in St. Mark's.

As mentioned, Carleen sings with a group called the Bach and Handel Chorale. A couple years ago the group had the chance to record some songs to make a professionally produced album. The acoustics and organ of the church provided the perfect recording studio. However, long cables had to be run from the microphones at the risers where the chorus was standing to the sound board and audio engineers capturing the recording in the "Great Hall" at the very back of the church. Given their choir director had to play the organ, he could not be standing in front of them to give queues and such. Therefore, the choir members had to pay close attention to their sheet music, which housed "breath marks" to synchronize their breaths and voices for each piece they performed. In order to reduce recording expenses, they were instructed to do one song after another. No retakes. No breaks. Get in, sing, record, and done.

94

As she was singing, Carleen noticed some movement in the back of the church. Her eyes lifted from her sheet music to focus on this movement. She saw an old woman and wondered if she were a grandmother to one of her fellow chorus members who snuck in to catch a glimpse of the recording session. Carleen resumed her focus on her sheet music; however, the old woman kept walking back and forth, ducking in and out from behind the two large pillars. Carleen knew she needed to focus on the music as they were told to capture the recording in one take, but this woman moving back and forth in her peripheral vision was so distracting and annoying. Finally, the old woman stood still in between the two pillars with her hands folded in front of her and watched the choir perform. There is a large, ornate, gold baptismal font in this part of the church and, from Carleen's vantage point, the woman was standing right in front of it, but not for too long. Carleen watched the woman dissolve from her view. It was at that point that Carleen realized she had been distracted the entire time by a ghost. Unsettling as this realization was, she maintained her professional composure and kept singing.

At the completion of the recording session, Carleen turned to her fellow choir members and asked: "Did anybody else see her?" Twelve others admitted to seeing the ghostly distraction. They convened and compared notes and descriptions of what they saw. They all saw this old woman wearing a full-length dark skirt, a white shirt that had ruffles around the collar and the wrists, a black shawl on her shoulders, her hair was in a bun, and she was wearing wire-rimmed eyeglasses.

Carleen theorizes that the power cables, microphones, and recording equipment might have given the spirit the "boost" it needed to manifest so solidly. I concur with this theory and would like to add that the singing carried a substantial weight of spiritual energy given its "positive vibrations."

A couple weeks later, the group had a performance scheduled at St. Mark's. They assembled and rehearsed with the orchestra. Once rehearsal was done, the group had some down time before the concert. Carleen asked a fellow choir member who provides tours of the church to give her the tour. The woman agreed and off they went touring the church. They arrived at this particular door that is always locked and Carleen wondered aloud as to what is behind that door as she's never been able to get back there. The tour guide had the key to the door and said: "Follow me." They entered a vestibule, which led to a smaller chapel. On the wall in the vestibule was a picture of a woman. Carleen only took one look and exclaimed: "That's her! That's the woman I saw during our recording session. Who is she?" The tour guide answered: "Mary Packer."

In addition to this church sighting, Mary's ghost has been reported at the Harry Packer Mansion, her brother's house, which today is a bed & breakfast. Guests say they have woken up in the middle of the night to see this old woman standing next to the foot of their bed. Some report that Mary actually leans over and stares directly at them. The following morning when the guests report the previous night's encounter to the concierge, they are shown a picture of Mary Packer Cummings and they positively identify her as the ghost in their room.

Sunday services are at 8:00 a.m. and 9:30 a.m. All are welcome. Whether one attends for the Holy Ghost or the Packer ghost, the 9:30 a.m. service has the full choir. The choice is yours.

CHAPTER 17

Living in a Haunted House, Bushkill, Pennsylvania

Homeowners endure the spirited company of several ghosts.

e Poconos

Leaving an apartment in Allentown, Pennsylvania, Joey, age fifty-one, and Greg, age forty-nine, purchased the "fixer-upper" home in Bushkill, Pennsylvania. They moved in October 1, 2006. Today, the modular house is approximately forty years old. The land on which it sits is much older.

Joey had his first encounter with the supernatural in the Allentown apartment. He told me: "One night Greg and I were talking in bed and I was lying on my side facing him. All of the sudden out of nowhere, something slapped on the mattress right behind my back. The slapping sound was audible. I jumped up but didn't see anyone there." Greg asked: "What was that?" There was enough residual lighting in the room from the streetlights outside the windows that if a person were there, Joey would have seen him.

As they began the process of moving, they moved boxes from the apartment to the house over several trips. Joey recalls they were putting packed moving boxes in the basement. As he passed the corner of the basement he felt a strong presence there. After he placed the box on the floor and turned to leave, the feeling was gone. He anxiously told Greg about what he sensed in the basement and hoped that whatever was in their apartment would stay behind at the apartment.

From time to time, Joey and Greg will smell cigar and cigarette smoke in the house. Joey is an ex-smoker, but Greg still smokes, but never in the house. Sometimes they smell perfume. These paranormal odors are there long enough for them to identify the scent and then they disappear.

Joey recalls the time they were in the basement with their dogs while the laundry was in the dryer upstairs. The dryer reached the end of its cycle and chimed to signal it was done. Immediately after this chiming, they heard footsteps above them that were proceeding via the dining room on their way to the laundry room. After validating no one had gained access to their home, they were disappointed that the ghost did not sort and fold the laundry.

In 2014, Joey was in the computer room working. Greg was down at the other end of the house. Joey heard a loud crash, and he got up to inspect the source of the sound. He found the metal folding door was ripped from its track and lying across the hallway diagonally. Greg came rushing towards the scene and said he heard the sound of the door being ripped from its track and crashing to the floor. But, he also heard Joey's voice saying "F--- off!" Greg asked Joey point blank: "Did you just say 'F--- off' to me?" Joey told him: "Absolutely not! I was in the computer room working. I didn't say anything. I heard this crash—same as you!"

This is the bi-fold door that was ripped from its track and thrown across the hallway by unseen hands. It remains leaning against the wall of the laundry room.

Joey noticed an expression on Greg's face that was very unsettling. He'd never seen Greg appear so cross. Greg admitted that he had this thought to take his gun out and shoot their dogs, Joey, and himself. Joey went down to the room where Greg keeps his lockbox and, sure enough, the box was open with the gun in plain sight. Joey took preventative measures to eradicate any further negativity in the home. He smudged (a Native American tradition of burning a white sage bundle or wand to clear away "psychic lice" and negative energy) the house, the property, and Greg. Using candles and crystals, Joey worked to seal the white light into the home. Thankfully, these measures worked and they haven't experienced anything so destructive and frightening since.

However, the home is not completely void of paranormal activity. It's not threatening or harmful, but it is there nonetheless. Joey and Greg hear voices conversing at times when they know for certain they are alone in the house. Joey described it as having a television on in a distant room of the house. He can hear the chatter but cannot discern what the dialogue is actually.

Friends of Joey's have witnessed the spirit activity as well. He met them at the Welcome Center off Route 80, just over the border in Pennsylvania, to lead them to his home. After pulling in the driveway, parking the cars, and convening on the front lawn with Greg and the dogs, the friends asked: "Who's in your house?" Joey and Greg answered: "No one. We're standing right here." Well, all three of the guests pointed to the bedroom window and said that is where they saw someone peeking out at them. This particular bedroom is the room where Greg's father used to stay when he came to visit. Greg's father had recently passed away.

Later that day, Joey's friend was in the living room while his sister and her husband were in the dining room speaking with Joey. Joey had his back to the living room. His friend's sister was facing the living room. Suddenly, Joey's friend in the living room said: "Oh shit!" He proceeded quickly from the living room and went outside. Joey asked his friend's sister: "What happened?" She replied: "I saw it too!" What she and her brother saw was a young boy staring out the front window of the living room. The boy turned away quickly from the window and went downstairs. Greg, who was in the basement, came running upstairs and asked: "What happened? Did you see the boy? Because he just walked into the basement."

Joey went outside to calm his friend. In the process of that conversation, the friend described the ghost in detail. When they returned inside, Greg and Joey's friend's sister gave the exact same description of the apparition.

Greg described the boy as a Native American teenager. However, this wasn't the first time Greg had seen the teen ghost. Greg went on to admit that this ghost spoke to him on several occasions. Although Greg cannot discern what the spirit was saying, it is doing its best to talk with him. In fact, Joey remembers the time Greg was talking to him and mid-sentence Greg stopped and turned as if he were being interrupted by someone. Joey could not see anyone there, and asked Greg to finish his sentence. Greg then clarified that the young Native American spirit was standing there and speaking to him. Joey

100

said to Greg: "Either you're a really great actor or this is really happening."

Joey often gets the feeling of not being alone, when he knows for a fact he is alone in the house. He said he'll be doing dishes and can sense someone walking up from behind him. He turns to look and, of course, no one is there. Lately, though, he finds that he is getting used to these feelings and more comfortable or accepting of the otherworldly presence in the house. That's not to say he doesn't keep his sage wand and crystals handy. Routine cleansings are *de rigueur*.

Ghosts are locality based, meaning they usually stay in their place or haunt. However, sometimes they travel. Sometimes they are mistaking the light of a person's aura as The Light or they recognize an emotional chord in a person that they resonate with, and they end up following that person to their home. I suspect the latter is the case for Joey. He and Greg were visiting fellow ghost hunter John Hotchkiss. While at John's house, Joey remarked that he sensed a male energy present. John was impressed with Joey's intuitive ability and confirmed having such a "roommate."

Later that night, back at their home, Greg and Joey were in the kitchen. Joey went to turn around while talking to Greg and saw a man standing in their kitchen. Joey described the man as Caucasian, tall, and thin with short dark hair that was combed perfectly in place. The man was wearing a dark suit and was staring at Joey and Greg. In the time it took for Joey to register what he was seeing, the apparition took a step towards the front door and vanished.

Joey called John and described what he had just seen. John confirmed that was exactly what his "roommate" looked like. Apparently, the ghost wanted to see where Joey and Greg live and then return to his haunt at the Hotchkiss'. That was the only time this spirit came to visit them.

There is a bedroom that Joey keeps closed off for the most part in the house because he senses, for lack of a better description, a portal in the one corner of this room. His friend's sister, who saw the Native American ghost boy while at Joey's house, also sensed this portal and intense energy emanating from the same corner of this bedroom. While it provides Joey some sense of relief that someone else senses this portal, it also validates his apprehension about going into this room.

This portal is somehow working like a doorway between our world and the spirit world. On a separate occasion, Joey was standing in the hallway close to the kitchen and he saw the spirit of a man come out of the bathroom and walk directly through the wall opposite the bathroom door. The room on

The beautiful Saw Creek that passes through Joey and Greg's backyard.

the other side of that wall is the bedroom with the portal.

There is one more notable spirit who is seen on occasion in the basement of the home. Joey described this man as short and stocky with a round face, salt and pepper, thick wavy hair and a bushy mustache. Joey was on the landing of the staircase when he saw this ghost man walk past the doorway of the basement. The ghost was fixated ahead and did not notice Joey standing on the landing above him. Joey ran down the stairs to see where the ghost went, but it was gone . . . vanished completely. When Joey asked Greg: "Have you seen the ghost guy?" Greg replied: "You mean the short, round guy in the basement?" Talk about positive identification and confirmation. Joey never said where he saw the ghost guy when he queried Greg.

It's interesting to note that a creek runs through the backyard of Joey and Greg's home. There's nothing like a water source to amplify spirit activity; couple that with the Lenni-Lenape Native American residual energies and the result is "Para Central Station." Fortunately, these "visitors" do not overstay their welcome or take up too much space.

CHAPTER 18

Jorgenson's at the Dimmick Inn

See mirror reflections of patrons not visible to the human eye . . . and more!

e Pocono

The original home of Samuel Dimmick was built in 1828. A devastating fire destroyed the home in 1854. His daughter, Frances, was determined to rebuild, and so she did. The reconstructed edifice housed twenty-five hotel rooms, a bar, and dining room. Over the years, the Dimmick Inn was the Milford Post Office and stagecoach stop. Additionally, it functioned as a boardinghouse, a deli, a Chinese restaurant, a brothel, and cabaret.

Purchasing the property in 2008, on the corner of Main and Broad Streets, Mary and Mike Jorgenson brought a fresh vitality to the place. Adding their surname to the title of the establishment, Jorgenson's at the Dimmick Inn, did not impress nor distress the locals who still refer to the place as "The Dimmick." The menu is chiefly American fare with burgers, paninis, and salads. The bar has commemorative dollar bills posted along the upper wall and ceiling. This practice reminded me of McSorley's Old Ale House in New York City with its chandelier coated with wishbones from young men who went off to fight in World War I. Mike and Mary are from Brooklyn, New York, and the Yankees memorabilia lovingly displayed throughout the bar drives that point home.

When my husband and I stopped in, we were greeted by Lisa Ryan, bartender. She graciously took time from her busy bar to talk with us about her ghostly experiences while working at the Dimmick since 2011. For the most part, the ghosts and their pranks do not bother her. However, this one particular time unnerved her. She was at the small bar just outside the dining room. In her head she was thinking: "Close that door. I don't want to see what's there." The door she was wishing was closed was the swinging one that allowed passage in and out of the formal dining area. She can't explain it, but for some reason she felt a presence there, by that doorway. Sometimes the feeling was so strong, she thought if she looked in that direction she would see a ghost standing there. This was one of those times where the feeling was intense, so much so that she had goosebumps forming on her forearms. She refused to look at the door, and then, suddenly, the door slammed shut.

Later, when the bar and restaurant were crowded, she mustered the bravery required for her to approach the door. She found the rubber stopper three inches from the threshold of the door on the bar room side. Lisa knows that she had that stopper tucked under the door holding it open on the dining room side. She retrieved the stopper and placed it under the door once again holding the door open. Lisa then tested the positioning of the stopper by pulling on the door. She tried

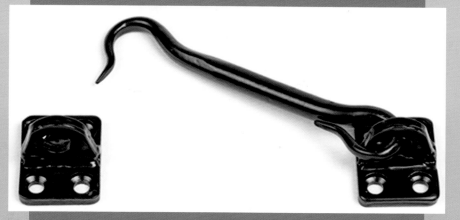

Example: Eyehook latch.

with all her strength to get that door to budge. It did not move. What force was capable of casting the stopper through the doorway to the bar room and slamming this door shut?

Her husband resided at the Dimmick in 2010. He told her about his experience wherein he locked the door to the attic before going to bed, and in the morning discovered it unlatched. Just to be clear, this was an old eyehook latch. There is no mistaking if one has correctly latched it or not given gravity contributes to the successful latching. I experienced this same instance at the General Wayne Inn in the early 1990s. In the ladies' room, the stall doors were to be brought together and then the eyehook would line up with the loop so one could connect them and thereby latch the doors for privacy. I latched them perfectly and hung my purse on the hook provided on the stall wall. When I was taking my purse from the wall hook, the doors—that I had not unlatched as yet—swung open. I stepped toward the sinks, and was confronted with an unbearable cold. Opting for my hand sanitizer in my purse, I skipped washing my hands and exited immediately. Later the bartender clued me in about their "Pervert Ghost," who either hangs out in the ladies' room or by the bar pinching unsuspecting female patrons, who then turn and slap the man within their reach.

The Dimmick has its share of SOP (Standard Operating Procedure) hauntings. Disembodied footsteps and other inexplicable sounds are heard by the employees and co-owner, Mike Jorgenson. Cold spots, such as in the supply room are felt. Electrical disturbances plague the paper towel dispenser to where it runs on its own and wastes a lot of paper towels. This may be the result of a ghost wanting to wash his or her etheric hands as the water in this same restroom runs on its own as well. The unsettling feeling of being watched or not alone is felt by various employees throughout the establishment. Most suspect the ghost to be that of Frances Dimmick, or "Fan," as she is affectionately known.

Tim, who conducts the town's ghost walks said: "The Dimmick is the most actively haunted building in Milford. There have been several events that have been witnessed by three or more people at one time. Some of these include objects moving or being thrown, noises, lights turning on and off repeatedly, and electrical devices turning on during power outages. Unseen hands are responsible for the flushing of toilets, opening and closing of doors, and turning on the water faucets."

Mike remembers the time he was seated at the bar having his morning coffee and watching the news. He was alone, or so he thought. He glanced in the mirror that hangs behind the bar and swore he saw someone standing right behind him. He whipped around in his chair to see who it was, and no one was there—well, not physically.

On a separate occasion, Mike witnessed the glasses that were piled neatly on the end of the bar slide off and crash to the floor. There was no one standing near them—no violent vibrations that would have caused them to fall. It was very strange. Lisa, however, offers the practical explanation of condensation and an uneven floor. Without testing this for myself, I cannot say for sure. A test would have to employ the documented variables of the height of the pile of glasses, the degree at which the floor slants, the direction of the slant, and the amount of condensation present on the glassware.

Whether or not an EVP is captured or specter is reflected in the bar's mirror, the food and drink make The Dimmick Inn a worthy stop on one's tour of the paranormal.

CHAPTER 19

Pennsylvania Dutch Lore— the Siwweyaeger

The Poconos' "Jersey Devil" equivalent.

The Pennsylvania Dutch are rooted throughout the Poconos and Lehigh Valley regions as well as in the southern central areas of Pennsylvania. It would be a huge oversight on my part not to touch on the culture and its superstitions. As a paranormal investigator, it is important, I feel, to know the traditions and beliefs of the people for whom you're providing an investigation. Not only will it save the investigator time in the research, but may help avoid coming across as insulting or insensitive while on the case.

In terms of the Pocono region, the Native American tribe dominating this area was the Lenni-Lenape. According to Living Places.com: "The tribe consisted of three principal subtribes: The Unami or Wonamey, the Minsi or Munsee, and the Unalachtigo or Unalatka, each having its own territory and slightly different dialect. According to Lenape tradition, they had migrated into eastern Pennsylvania from the west, the tribal divisions later receiving their names from some geographic or other peculiarity characterizing the region in which they lived."

When the Dutch arrived, they cooperated and co-existed peacefully, for the most part, with the local Native Americans. However, over time and via various land acquisitions by the British and the Dutch, tensions grew and battles were fought. Legend says that the Native Americans killed a Dutch family, save for the mother. For revenge, she performed Hexerie, a Penn-Dutch form of witchcraft, and created the Siwweyeager. In German "jäger," literally means "huntsman," from *jagen* "to hunt." For all intents and purposes, she created a "death spirit." But, magic is not foolproof, and the Siwweyeager decided it would kill Dutchmen in peacetime and kill their enemies in wartime.

The Siwweyeager appeared as a hunter with huge wings, and he carried a long flintlock rifle. He dressed in buckskins and wore moccasins on his feet, but there was a Dutch influence to the remainder of his clothing. He was seen primarily in Blue Mountain, Stony Mountain, and Second Mountain areas of Pennsylvania. When he would fly or hover over a particular home, within a week's time someone in that home would die. (This is similar to what my grandmother used to tell me about owls. She said that if an owl lands on the roof of a home and hoots, it portends death to someone who lives there.) Andrew K. told me: "I'm Pennsylvania Dutch, but I was adopted, so I didn't have a lot of firsthand knowledge about it. However, in Pennsylvania we have figures like the Pennsylvania Dutch Dragons. Supposedly there were dragon sightings up to the early twentieth century." Needless to say, people were terrified of the Siwweyeager and considered it pure evil.

As for killing the Dutchmen's enemies in times of war, that was first realized in the American Revolutionary War. The Siwweyeager would hover over the head of a Hessian or British officer, and the Dutch patriot would take notice of this and simply shoot in that direction. Even at 400 yards the bullet would pass right through their hearts. During the Civil War, the Siwweyeager hovered over groups of Confederates who were trying to hide, thus exposing them.

When a war ended, the Siwweyeager would resume its "death spirit" or "reaper" role and collect souls of naughty people, such as runaway indentured servants, horse thieves, and moonshiners.

When a Sioux chief was consulted about the Siwweyeager, he said that Death is a constant companion. He believed that by getting clear with oneself, one would see his own personal Siwweyeager, and one should make friends with him. Knowing your Death Spirit in this way, allows for a gentle relationship wherein it will tell you when it's not your time, and will help you prepare when it is.

This is the Hex sign that hangs in the author's kitchen.

A Penn-Dutch Tradition: the Hex Sign

These colorful images appear on garages, barns, and above doors of houses. The name is derived from a misinterpretation. The six pointed star was a popular choice of Hex signs. Six is "sechs" in German, but was construed by the non-German speaking people as "hex." The colors and symbols all have meaning, such as birds and stars for good luck and hearts for love. Colors are as follows: White is purity; green is prosperity, red is strong emotion, and blue is protection.

CHAPTER 20

East Stroudsburg University

Major in academics and paranormal activity.

Ghosts of t

In the heart of East Stroudsburg is the beautiful campus of East Stroudsburg University. Originally opened as Normal School in 1893, today, it offers both undergraduate and graduate degree programs.

There are, however, a few buildings on campus that offer more than an academic experience. Over the years, several paranormal groups have investigated the purported hauntings of ESU.

Eric Pensyl has conducted the Ghost Fests every October for the past five years here. He brings all of his ghost hunting equipment so the students get to experience firsthand what it is like to be a ghost hunter. Items, such as the Mel Meter, EMF meter, and cell sensor are just a few of the pieces he employs on an investigation. After a brief presentation that covers the paranormal investigating basics and the target areas on campus, Eric divides the students into teams. The teams are dispatched to separate campus locations to investigate. He admits that there have been instances when one or two of the students got so scared, they had to leave before the investigation was completed.

At the Fine and Performing Arts Center allegedly resides the spirit of "Sarah," a former theater major at the university. She committed suicide by hanging herself from a light grid. Reports of cold spots and mysterious shadows on the catwalk are attributed to her.

It makes for a great story; however, the only ESU student named Sarah that I could find proof of death was a Sarah (last name not given out of respect for her family) who died subsequent to a car accident on December 24, 2007. She was a junior at ESU, and the news article did not list what her area of study was. Eric said he conferred with local police, and they had no record of any such suicide in this building. In any event, a séance was conducted and the Ghost Fest participants sent the supposed spirit of "Sarah" to that great stage in the sky.

Behind the stage, Eric said his team made contact with the spirit of little boy named "Joe." The legend states that a construction worker brought his young son with him to work. The child fell down an elevator shaft and died. However, this legend is attached to the dorm of Hawthorne Hall. While no concrete evidence can be found to prove or disprove this legend, the fact remains that the elevator in Hawthorne Hall opens and closes its doors all by itself.

Eric's crew then ventured into the Abeloff building. He noted that most of the paranormal activity takes place on or around the stage area. The team determined that the spirit of "Joshua" was present. Via a series of questions and answers derived from

The Fine and Performing Arts Center where a séance was held to release the theater's ghost named Sarah.

watching a flashlight centered in the room turn on and off—by itself, the students participating in the flashlight Q&A discovered that "Joshua" was a former teacher at ESU who drowned in the flood of 1955.

After extensive research into the flood that claimed more than seventy lives in August of 1955, not one corroborating piece of evidence could support this conclusion. There was a campground called the Davis Camp. Forty-four lives were lost when a wall of water, thirty feet high, flooded from the Brodcreek into the camp within fifteen minutes. Mostly women and children were here except for two men. Was "Joshua" one of those men? There are no records that I can find to answer this question. It should also be noted that East Stroudsburg University sits up high enough so that it was not tragically affected from this flood as the lower lying areas were.

I asked Eric about the flashlight investigative technique. I've seen this done on television shows and dismissed it as ridiculous. He said that he thought the same thing about it initially. However, he found if he unscrewed the flashlight and then screwed it back together so the contacts are barely touching, it would allow for

The Abeloff Center for the Performing Arts.

the ghost to muster enough telekinetic energy to turn the light on and off.

Sorry, the skeptic in me is still not warm to this whole process. It would not take much of a vibration for the contacts to graze each other and thereby produce a flash of light. Sound is vibration. What if the very question being asked carries with it enough tonal vibration that the contacts in the light meet and turn the flashlight on for a moment? Then again, there is the basic physics of expansion and contraction. The heating and cooling process of the metal inside the flashlight is affected by the temperature of the bulb. Therefore the cycle of on and off can repeat continuously.

Eric asked how many people are in the room and began counting, the flashlight turned on at the number thirty. And, lo and behold, there were thirty people in the room. This exemplifies coincidence. However, this does not explain what he tested next. Using four different colored flashlights, he asked the ghost to touch a particular colored flashlight such as the red one or the blue one, and that corresponding colored flashlight turned on. He then asked if the ghost would turn on all four flashlights simultaneously, and it did just that. Eric said that they documented concurrent hits on other equipment such as the Mel meter or cell sensor when the flashlights lit up. Sometimes he recorded an EVP at the same time the light came on.

I'll admit the last two tests give me pause to want to examine this further on my own, but I do caution investigators against straying from "yes" and "no" questions, especially when using this method or the K-2 method. Both these methods are operating along the lines of the Spiritualism movement's "Table Tipping" or "Table Rapping." Table Tipping had the ghost levitate the table's designated side for "yes" and the other designated side for "no." Table Rapping used one rap (knock) for "yes" and two raps (knocks) for "no." It is very easy to get carried away with these communication methods and edit the questions to create one's own romantic tale. I must also caution the reader that these methods are in the same family as the talking boards. Every case I have ever investigated that crossed the line from a simple ghost haunting to a demonic level always traced back to someone in the household having played the talking board. I prefer an EVP session so that the ghost can relay their own message.

When the team visited Shawnee Hall, a dorm on campus, they were told the legend of a janitor who died in the basement, possibly a suicide. To this day, one can hear his keys jingling as well as other muffled voices emanating from that section of the basement. Eric's teammate addressed the spirit by saying: "Did you commit suicide? It's a shame. We're sorry that happened." A chilling EVP was recorded in response. The guttural voice responded with: "Enough! Leave me alone!" Again, no proof exists to say this was the ghostly janitor replying, but whoever is down in that basement definitely does not want company.

Aside from the buildings investigated during the Ghost Fests, there are other spots on and off campus that have a spooky tale to tell. Kemp Library is known to have the spirit of a cat roaming about the government documents section in the lower level of the library. I spoke with Assistant Professor Ramona Hylton who said she has not seen the ghostly cat, but has seen something from the corner of her eye dart by when working in that section. I investigated this area with camera and digital audio recorder, but did not capture any evidence of the phantom feline.

Two fraternity houses are known for their ghosts. Phi Sigma Kappa, at 91 Analomink Street, is home to "Mrs. Booth." Her ashes are said to be buried beneath the fireplace. As a result, Mrs. Booth is seen as a glowing apparition near the fireplace or sometimes manifesting on the second and third floors. I interviewed Ted and Kim Markou, of Markou Paranormal, who captured a

Kemp Library where the ghost cat appears.

golden glowing specter on video while investigating this frat house. They attribute their anomaly to be that of Mrs. Booth. While searching for a positive identification of Mrs. Booth, I found a Mrs. Sarah Booth who lived in Stroudsburg at the time of the 1940 Census. She was seventy-six years old at that time having been born in 1864. I could not determine her exact address, but seeing Stroudsburg and not East Stroudsburg listed, I can safely assume this is not the same Mrs. Booth of Phi Sigma Kappa.

The other fraternity that has a spirit is Sigma Pi on the corner of Smith and Analomink Streets. The fraternity brothers refer to her as "Margie." While the story of Margie is embellished for the annual trick-or-treaters who want candy from the "haunted house," the handed-down version goes as follows: Margie was a housekeeper and had an affair with the master of the house. Once this affair came to light, she was punished by being sequestered in the tiny room on the third floor. She lived out her days in that room, and after she died, her cremated remains were stored in an urn that was placed in that room and then walled off from the rest of the house. Years later, some fraternity brothers

Fraternity house of Sigma Pi reportedly has the ghost of "Margie."

decided to expand the living space and began knocking down the wall. During this demolition, the urn fell and broke open scattering the ashes on the floor. Shortly thereafter, the haunting ensued. The telephone would ring in an unusual pattern, items fell to the floor for no reason, and there were uncomfortable feelings and cold spots sensed by brothers and their visitors throughout the large Victorian house. The Old Hag Syndrome was experienced by the fraternity brother who attempted to spend the night in the crawl-space that is at the peak of the house. To clarify, the Old Hag Syndrome is a form of narcolepsy wherein the brain does not re-engage certain muscles in the body as the person is awakening. This is experienced as paralysis. Sometimes it is coupled with hallucinations because the brain has not disengaged from the dream state.

For the most part, the fraternity brothers do not mind Margie; some view her as the House Mother who watches over them.

East Stroudsburg University does not offer parapsychology in any of its curricula, but it does provide the experiential laboratory in the form of paranormal activity.

CHAPTER 21

Ghost That Goes Bang in Bangor

(A Private Haunted Home)

Hear a noisy ghost of an otherwise quiet town.

The movie *Poltergeist*, released in 1982, depicted a family terrorized by the spirits of those whose bodies were buried beneath the newly constructed homes of the Cuesta Verde development. This was loosely based on the Black Hope Curse of San Antonio, Texas. There, a subdivision was built over the unmarked graves of former black slaves. Granted, a large demonic head did not burst forth from anyone's closet like in the movie, but furniture moving on its own and bodies being discovered when digging to install an in-ground swimming pool did.

Bangor is quite the misnomer as the town itself is a quiet slice of suburbia in the Poconos. Well, it is quiet except for this one-half of a duplex home. Former resident Kimberly V. detailed in an interview her harrowing experience.

Kim moved in with her boyfriend and his two daughters in November 2013. Unsettling things began to happen almost immediately. Day three of living there, Kim and the girls were downstairs, and her boyfriend was at work. She thought she heard water running in the upstairs bathroom. She went up to inspect and found no water running. She then went into the girls' bedroom and found their alarm clock playing white noise. This accounted for the sound of running water, but did not explain how the clock was activated. Both girls were still downstairs and the alarm feature clearly was not set. Kim pulled the plug of the clock from the wall socket and the noise stopped.

Later, while still unpacking from the move, Kim was putting things away in the closet of her bedroom. The girls were asleep in the bedroom next to hers with the door closed. Suddenly, the door of their bedroom slammed open so hard that it bounced off the wall. The girls remained asleep, but the dog started barking incessantly, and its fur was standing on end. Kim took off downstairs. She texted her boyfriend at work and told him: "There's something going on here. The girl's bedroom door just slammed open, and I don't know why." He texted back: "Are you sure?" She replied: "Yes, I'm sure. The kids are asleep and the door is not loose in any way that would cause it to slam like that."

A few nights later, her boyfriend's ex-wife came by to pick up the girls to take them to dinner. As she was retrieving something from her car, she noticed the light in the window of Kim's bedroom flicking on and off five consecutive times. When she went inside the home, she asked Kim if she was just upstairs. Kim said: "No, I've been down here helping the girls get ready to go with you. Why?" The ex-wife told Kim what she had seen with the light going on and off in the window. Again, the ex said: "Are you sure you weren't up there?" This time the girls, who were three and five years old, confirmed that Kim was with them the whole time. Kim asked the ex: "Are you sure you saw the lights go and off?" The ex-wife replied with certainty: "Yes. I stood there and watched and they turned on and off several times while wondering to myself, 'what the hell is she is doing?'" After the girls left with their mother, Kim went upstairs to make sure the light switch was indeed in the "off" position and that no one was up there.

On another occasion, her boyfriend—who sleeps very soundly—awoke from a noise he'd heard. He had to rustle Kim awake to ask her: "Did you hear that?" She had not heard anything. He repeated his question and added: "Didn't you feel that? There's something in here." She didn't know what to make of the situation, although he was definitely frightened. He was actually shaking. That scared her as this was a man who never got spooked or frightened by anything before.

They proceeded to go downstairs and check to see if someone had broken in. After searching the basement, first floor, and attic, it was obvious that no one else was in the house. This was the only time he'd experienced something like this in the house. The rest of the time the activity focused on Kim, the dog, and the kids.

This activity continued for a month, and Kim refused to go upstairs alone. The girls' bedroom door would periodically repeat its action of slamming open. Eventually, Kim and her boyfriend employed an old baby monitor with a built-in viewing screen. They positioned the camera to face into the girls' bedroom while they kept vigil at the monitor downstairs.

One night, the younger girl—"B"—got out of her bed and appeared to be in a trance. Kim and her boyfriend drew close to the monitor to see the child standing and rocking back and forth in the middle of her room. She was mumbling as if carrying on a conversation with someone. B had never sleepwalked and was never diagnosed as having night terrors.

Unable to watch any longer, Kim and her boyfriend ran upstairs to confront the little girl. As they entered the room, B looked at them and simply said: "I'm playing with my friend." They inquired: "Who's your friend?" B replied: "I can't tell you. It's a secret."

Later that night, when they went to bed, Kim's boyfriend fell fast asleep. She was wide awake and needed to watch television in bed until she could go to sleep. By 3:00 a.m., she noticed the door to their bedroom was swinging back and forth. As she looked more closely, she saw the black shadow of a man who was making the door move. She could not determine clothing, hair, or eye color—just that he was about six-feet-five inches tall. She woke her boyfriend up and asked him if he saw the shadow. He confirmed that he saw the door swinging on its own, but did not see any shadow man. Kim said: "He's staring right at me! You don't see him?" With that her boyfriend yelled at the shadow: "Go away!" But, it did not leave. She cowered under the covers and did not come out from under them until the next morning.

By February 2014, Kim reached out to a local paranormal investigative team to help her. The team concluded that this was the spirit of an older man from the town of Bangor who was acting in a protective manner where Kim was concerned. The team placed the name of this spirit as "Richard" and said that he was protective of Kim because in life he failed at protecting someone he loved. Perhaps this was the emotional chord that was struck when Kim moved in that spurred on the poltergeist activity. The team also determined the spirit of a little eight-year-old boy named Oliver was the secret friend of B.

How the team arrived at these conclusions is not clear to Kim, but she did say that her neighbor on the other side of the wall of the duplex had experienced ghostly activity as well. The neighbor's son reported seeing the ghost boy and the neighbor had her arm scratched by invisible fingernails.

Since her boyfriend was a professional DJ, he had top of the line recording equipment. They decided to set up the recorder one night before they left to go shopping. When they returned and played the recording back, they heard a man's voice talking to their dog saying: "Hi puppy. Hi puppy." Then they heard the voice of a little boy asking: "What's that?" followed by the voice of a woman stating: "You got to be kidding me." Kim confirmed the voices were not that of her neighbors.

Their dog was left in the kitchen and had access to go upstairs, but would not be able to get past the metal baby gate that was installed at the top of the stairs. Yet, in the recording, they heard the gate being jiggled and the button to release the gate was being pressed. Thankfully, the spirit was not strong enough to open the gate as this was installed to prevent the kids from falling down the stairs if they got up in the middle of the night. Additionally on the recording, the dog sounded very excited as if he saw someone.

Dangerous poltergeist activity proceeded with candles lighting themselves. The first time it happened was right after Kim had had a dream about her mother, who passed away in 2007. In the dream, her mother wanted her to light a candle.

Kim was overwhelmed by the fact that she could feel her mother's touch during the dream. When she woke from the dream she tried to tell her boyfriend, but he was sound asleep. She drifted back to sleep as well. Later, her boyfriend got up to take the girls to school. Before he left, he woke Kim to ask her if she had gotten up in the middle of the night to light a candle. She said: "No. Why?" He told her that he found a candle lit in the kitchen when he first went downstairs. Another time a candle was found lit on its own was when they returned home on Easter Sunday. This candle was in the dining room.

After the team completed their paranormal investigation, Kim noticed the activity subsided tremendously. She took time to research the property and found that the house was constructed as a single-family home in the early 1920s. A man in his seventies died of natural causes in what was now her bedroom of the house. As best as she could determine, the house was split in two sometime during the 1970s.

Kim has since moved out of the house and that relationship. She happily resides with her new beau in the Bethlehem area. She's very thankful that the spirits and their activities did not move with her.

Kim's First Encounter with the Paranormal

Kim's parents bought their family home off Shafer's School House Road in Stroudsburg back in 1985. The house itself was constructed in 1980. Her mother was the first to experience the energy of the house as it drained her of her own energy. She got "sick" while living there. She was very lethargic. Kim's mother went from one doctor to the next only to be told there was nothing wrong with her.

One day, Kim was playing with her toy kitchen set in the dining room. She could see her mother seated at the kitchen table cutting vegetables on the cutting board. Suddenly, the gray sweater her mother was wearing caught fire. There were no open flames, cigarettes, or candles lit anywhere near her mother. Kim's mother jumped up from the table and dashed to the kitchen sink while stripping off the sweater. By the time she threw the sweater in the sink and turned the water on, there were no flames—no burn marks, no remnants of smoke. Her mother was not burned or injured. This was perplexing.

As a little girl, Kim would frequently tell her mother "Boo behind you!" This meant Kim was seeing a man standing right behind her mother—and he wasn't her father. In fact, he was a man unknown to Kim.

Since her father was the general manager of The Shawnee Inn at this time, he was friends with one of the Native Americans who held their annual PowWows at the resort. This shaman visited Kim's mother at their home and determined there was a spirit of an elderly Native American attached to her. He was draining the life out of her mother. Fortunately, this shaman was able to detach the spirit and release her mother from its grip. To this day, Kim and her father have no idea how this Indian spirit became attached to her mother.

Sadly, Kim's mother passed away from brain and lung cancer in 2007. She is buried in Sleepy Hollow, New York, where she was from originally. As a child, her mother used to play in this very cemetery. Kim's grandmother still lives in the same house next to the cemetery. It's possible that the Indian spirit attached itself to Kim's mother in her childhood, but didn't come to the fore until she moved into the house in Stroudsburg. The Native Americans dominant in the Sleepy Hollow area are Mohawk. Perhaps this Indian spirit sensed being in enemy Lenni-Lenape territory and needed to muster its strength by "vampiring" energy from Kim's mom.

In June 2006, at the age of fifteen, Kim had her most bizarre and frightening experience in the family's home. At 5:00 a.m., her mother came to wake her for school. As Kim woke up she noticed something in her mouth—like a "fuzz ball." As she attempted to pick this out from her mouth, she realized it was a not a piece of fuzz. She didn't know what it was. She turned on her light and saw that she was covered in blood, and it was actually a clot of blood in her mouth. Her bedspread had bloody handprints on it. Her hair was saturated with blood, and it had seeped all over her pillow, too. She screamed for her mom who arrived almost immediately to see this horrific sight. Her mother ran and woke Kim's father. They came to her room and her dad said: "She was not like that at 4:00 a.m. I checked her before I went to bed." To clarify, Kim's father got home around 2:00 a.m. from working late at The Shawnee Inn. After watching television to wind down, he checked on his daughter as he always did before going to bed.

Her parents helped her out of bed and began to examine her for any cuts or gashes. There were none. Carefully she cleaned herself off and her parents took her to the pediatrician to be examined professionally. He could find nothing wrong with her. Further, the blood sample retrieved from the pillowcase her mother brought to the doctor's office proved it was not Kim's blood. It wasn't her mother's or her father's blood, either. They had no idea as to whose blood it was. It's too bad the pictures Kim's mother took of this event are nowhere to be found.

When Kim was eighteen years old, she got locked in the basement. She had to wait for her dad to come home from work and let her out. He said to her: "How the hell did you get locked in the basement?" She thought to herself: "Yeah, really, how?" The basement door is screened to allow the heat from the basement stove to warm the first floor of the house. The door is secured by an eyehook latch. There is no way for this latch to fall right into the hoop without holding the door in place and lining up the loop with the eyehook. Plus, the latch is at the top of the door so it's impossible for someone to walk by and knock it in or out of the locked position.

This happened again to Kim while at her dad's house recently. She went down the basement and when she tried to get back upstairs the door was latched. Not having her cellphone with her and not wanting to sit in the basement for hours waiting for her dad to come home, she cut through the screen with a screwdriver she retrieved from her dad's workbench. She was then able to unlatch the door. Still, that was quite a struggle for her as she's five-feet-four inches in height and the latch is at the top of the door at floor level. She had to stand on the tips of her toes and wield the screwdriver upwards to unlatch the lock.

Kim's experiences rank up there with an episode of the television show *Supernatural*. Having spoken with her at length, I can assure you she is a stable, intelligent young woman. For all my years in the paranormal field, writing her chapter (and Donny Decker's chapter) were the only times I was unnerved— well, okay, scared. I needed to step away from the computer to process and detach.

CHAPTER 22

Pocono Cinema and Cultural Center

The phantom of the theater strikes again.

owntown East Stroudsburg has its "Main Street USA" shops and eateries. In the heart of this bustling little town is the Pocono Cinema and Cultural Center. The building dates back to 1884 and then housed the Academy of Music, which was a vaudeville theater. Later it was titled the Grand Opera House. With the advent of "moving pictures," it became a movie house in 1913—the very first one in Monroe County. Tragically, the 1929 fire devastated the theater, but it did not completely destroy it. Its successful restoration saw its "rebirth" in January 1930.

During the 1940s and 1950s, the theater provided the community with newsreels and entertaining movies. However, by 1986, the theater was closed. It sat abandoned until 1996, when John and Carolyn Yetter purchased it and began renovations. They renamed the theater the Pocono Cinema and successfully ran the operation until the early 2000s by showing "artsy and indy" films. When they were ready to retire from the movie theater business, some of their employees rallied together to keep the place going. They managed for less than a year to keep it afloat. The Yetters returned for their "command performance" of six months and the theater shut its doors once more.

By 2008, the nonprofit theater model was proposed by Raymond Scheetz and Dan Dunn. Similar to the County Theater in Doylestown, Pennsylvania, the newly named Pocono Community Theater incorporated the artsy-indy films that the Yetters cherished, but also played the current films to attract patrons. But, by 2015, Scheetz and Dunn departed the theater's company. Under new management the theater's name changed to the Pocono Cinema and Cultural Center. As a nonprofit, volunteer labor and monetary donations aid the day-to-day operations and keep the ticket prices affordable for theatergoers. Some of the movie events include catering by local restaurants. For example, the theater ran the holiday screen classic *It's a Wonderful Life* with dinner and ice cream included in the ticket price of only $10.

Tyler Kittle has worked at the theater for the past three years as its projectionist. Tyler is a bright young man who also works on the local squad as an EMT (emergency medical technician). He explained that movies no longer arrive on reels, but in DCPs—Digital Cinema Package, which looks like a small hard drive. Once the drive is placed in the computer-based projector, the projectionist "builds" the movie from the files, which takes, on average, an hour.

In terms of the ghosts and the paranormal, Tyler said most of the occurrences happen when he's alone in the projection room. Doors will slam—and there's no breeze whatsoever in that area to force a door to slam; lights go on or shut off for no reason.

Tyler recalled the time while in the employee kitchen prepping his lunch, he thought he'd heard Luke, who works in the theater's café, ask him a question. Tyler proceeded to answer, but when he turned to face

Luke, he saw no one there. He went downstairs and Luke was behind the concession stand counter. Tyler asked: "Weren't you just upstairs, talking to me?" Luke replied: "No, why? I was talking to you down here." Basically Luke thought Tyler was at the front desk in the lobby, and Tyler thought Luke was upstairs with him in the employee lunch room.

Sometimes there is an inexplicable heaviness in certain areas of the theater according to Tyler. "You just know you're not alone sometimes. Things go missing and reappear in odd places of the theater, too."

In the summer of 2014, a theater patron encountered a ghost. Tyler explained: "We have three shows: 4:00, 7:00 and 10:00 p.m. A lady arrived to see the 10:00 p.m. show and was the only one—she had theater three all to herself." Or, so she thought. Halfway through the movie, she came out to the lobby and told Tyler: "There's someone else in there." He assured her that she was the only person he sold a ticket to for that show. She continued: "I can feel him breathing from the seat right behind mine." Concerned that someone may have snuck into the theater, Tyler went to inspect. There was no one in there.

Later that same summer, the theater saw its first paranormal investigation. C.O.R.E. Phenomena arrived to investigate from 10:00 p.m. to 5:00 a.m. John Hotchkiss said: "Although it was a long time to be on site, it was a good use of the team's time. We documented EVPs and had a dramatic Frank's Box session that seemed to be the voice of one of Tyler's relatives coming through."

For those of you unfamiliar with Frank's Box, it was the instrumental trans-communication (ITC) device invented by Frank Sumption in 2002. Supposedly, while scanning the AM radio band, the device would pick up spirit voices and, in some instances, allow for a two-way communication between the living and the dead."

Theater three proved to be the most active during the investigation. Tyler recalled at one point, John was walking up the center aisle and asking for EVPs. Suddenly, there was a loud bang on the back wall of the theater—right behind where Tyler was standing. On the other side of this wall is a hallway. The team confirmed no one was in the hallway at that time.

During the course of John's research about the theater and its surrounding area, he found there were never any murders, deaths, or tragedies (save the 1929 fire) of any kind connected to the theater. However, he did learn that there are tunnels under the theater that extend down to where Frazetta's (costume store) is located and over to where the Dansbury Depot used to be. These tunnels, for the most part, are not traversable because of the water in them. However, it may be that underground water that is acting as a conduit and heightening the paranormal activity in the theater.

Either way, the Pocono Cinema and Cultural Center is a worthy stop on the tour for ghosts or simply to take in a movie.

CHAPTER 23

Honorable Mentions

Campfire ghosts: various local legends and lore.

e Poconos

Sometimes a good ghost story is just that—a story. The Poconos is home to many short and sweet, or in some cases, tragic ghost stories. Some of these locations do not exist anymore, or they are mere ruins, but the legends and/or stories merit telling.

Princess Winona

Princess Winona was the beautiful daughter of Lenni-Lenape Chief Wissinoming. The history of this story is first relayed in the book *The Delaware Water Gap, Its Legends and Early History* written by Luke W. Brodhead in 1870. Winona's story takes place in the 1600s when the Dutch were migrating down from New York to the Delaware Water Gap region. This was a peaceful time and Winona enjoyed visiting with the Dutch women and learning their customs.

When the chief, her father, died, tensions mounted between the Dutch and other Native tribes, especially concerning the Great Shawano Island and who was entitled to this fertile land. Topping this tension was the killing of a young, popular colonist. In an effort to maintain peace between her tribe and the Dutch, Winona offered the Dutch the Island of Manwallamink while the Lenape would retain Shawano. Further she offered to sacrifice her life in an attempt to even the score for the killing of the colonist. The latter offer was refused by the Dutch settlers as they simply adored her.

Hendrick Van Allen, who was supervising the copper mines in the area and farther north, heard of Princess Winona and made it a point to meet her. Their relationship started as friends and quickly grew to be much more. Sadly, Van Allen was ordered to return to Holland once the British took over the area of the mines. When he finally told Winona the news that he would be leaving, she ran towards the cliff. Knowing she was going to attempt suicide by leaping to her death, Van Allen ran after her. He caught her just before she jumped; but the rocky terrain made for unstable footing and they both tumbled over the edge to their death.

The legend states that they fell while maintaining their embrace. Today, the sight of two "balls of fire" cascading down the mountainside from the cliff is representative of these two lovers falling to their death centuries ago.

Flagstaff at Jim Thorpe

At the very top of Jim Thorpe is Flagstaff. Local lore says that during the Civil War a young man climbed to the top of the mountain and raised the United States flag from a tree that had been struck by lightning. Later, in 1901, a trolley was constructed to connect Mauch Chunk and Lehighton. The Ballroom at Flagstaff not only hosted premier weddings in the 1980s, but allowed for hang gliders to launch from its platform. Since 2007, Tim Markley, president of Surreal Properties, has been trying to get approval to further develop the property with the addition of a hotel. Originally he proposed a seventy-eight-room hotel, but as of July 2015, he has received conditional approval to construct a thirty-seven-room boutique hotel.

When I spoke with Amanda, the bartender at the Covered Bridge Inn, she told me about the time she was helping her father with a job at Flagstaff. Her father is a contractor and was hired to do some repair and minor construction work at the Ballroom. Amanda said her father was given the keys to the place so he would have access to work. Being protective, Amanda's father was careful to lock the doors while they were inside working. One day while working, both Amanda and her father heard footsteps on the lower level. Her father said: "Didn't you lock the door behind you?" Amanda was certain she had, but went downstairs to check. No one responded to her calls of "hello" as she descended the stairs. She made her way to the door, and sure enough, it was locked.

Amanda said hearing the disembodied footsteps every so often became commonplace, and she was comfortable with ignoring the sounds and continuing her work.

Pocono Manor

The Inn at Pocono Manor records its first guests checking in on August 16, 1902. At that time the inn was comprised of sixty-five guest rooms and operated as a seasonal resort. By November 1907, the inn completed construction of its "Winter Inn" making it a year-round resort. By 1925, 106 rooms were added via the "Black Tower Wing." The Donald Ross designed eighteen-hole golf course was completed in 1927. Today, the Inn at Pocono Manor commands 3,000 acres of beauty for weddings, reunions, and corporate gatherings. Guests can enjoy the Exchange restaurant's fine

Flagstaff Restaurant.

dining or the Laurel Spa for pampering. Ghost hunters can enjoy visiting with the guests who have not checked out as yet.

The first time my husband, Kent, and I went to the Exchange restaurant, we fell in love with it. The menu made it difficult to choose an entrée as they all sounded so good, but luckily we were both satisfied with our choices. After dinner, we strolled through the lobby of the hotel and down the hallway to find the restrooms. Even though I was not here in a ghost-hunter capacity, this stroll set off my internal "ghost-o-meter." I could not put my finger on what or why this was eerily familiar to me.

On the drive home, I mentioned this weird feeling to Kent and he confirmed that he'd experienced it as well. There was a moment of silence in our conversation and then in chorus we said: *The Shining*! Walking down that hallway was right out of Stanley Kubrick's movie.

Let's fast forward to working on this book and meeting the chef of the Tom X Pub. While talking about her ghostly experiences working at Tom X, she asked: "Have you been to Pocono Manor? That place is creepy—like *The Shining* creepy." I told her that I had been to the Pocono Manor only to dine, but wanted to investigate it for its haunted legacy given the experiences recounted to me by the bartender/waitress at Tom X and former employee of the Pocono Manor.

"Liz" (name changed to protect the identity of the former employee) was the shift captain for the breakfast rush. She arrived to the Exchange restaurant long before anyone else had arrived. She set up the coffee to brew for the lobby and proceeded to ready the restaurant. After breakfast, she was locking up and noticed a young girl sitting in one of the booths. Liz described the little girl as having a big bow in her hair, and she was rocking back and forth on the seat. Liz asked her: "What are you doing here all by yourself? Did your parents just leave you here?" The girl did not respond. Liz turned her attention back to locking the gate, but when she turned to look back, the little girl had vanished. Liz went to the front desk receptionist in the lobby and asked: "Did you see a little girl come through here?" The receptionist replied that she had not seen anyone, except Liz, come into the lobby at that time.

Another time Liz saw someone enter through the swinging door that leads to the kitchen. She went to the door and it was still moving slightly as if someone had pushed it open to pass through. She entered the kitchen through this same door, but no one was there. Again she asked at the front desk if they had seen anyone come in, and, again, the answer was "no."

Ghostly rumor has it that in the early 1900s a child fell down the basement steps and died. Today, the staff of the inn avoid going down to the basement after sunset. Although I researched this tragic story extensively, I could not find any proof to validate it.

I spoke with a bartender at the Pocono Manor's lounge, and she said she had not seen any ghosts, but on several occasions has heard the balls on the pool table being knocked around as if someone was playing pool. When she goes into the pool room, no one is there, and the table is completely undisturbed.

While Pocono Manor is picturesque in its architecture, and the views from the lounge and terrace ballroom are breathtaking, one cannot escape the eerie feeling that is pervasive—even on sunny days. If you choose to spend a weekend or longer there, try to get up extra early in the morning and take a stroll down to the Exchange restaurant. Perhaps the little ghost girl will be waiting there.

What remains of the Henryville Inn.

Henryville House

Originally built in 1842, Henry's Halfway House was the enterprise of J. Russell Henry. It became the fishing mecca of the Poconos, and later it morphed into one of the most cherished resorts in the Poconos. At the intersection of Routes 191 and 715, former presidents Theodore Roosevelt, Grover Cleveland, and Benjamin Harrison vacationed here.

Today the main guest house has been leveled and the remaining building is rotting away with its windows boarded up and "Do Not Cross—Private Property" yellow streamer tape encircling the corner property.

When I visited the site, it was broad daylight. I was careful not to cross the yellow tape and took a couple pictures from the roadside. I could hear a woman's voice yelling off in the distance, but I did not pay attention to it. After I was walking back to my car, I heard the shrill scream of this woman once more. I looked up the hill on Route 715 and there stood a post-menopausal woman waving her arms and yelling: "What are you doing? That's private property. You have no right to be there!" Maybe it was the long hours spent writing this book, or the insufficient IV drip of caffeine, or the plain old "Jersey Girl" in me, but I responded with: "You talking to me?" (De Niro, you would have been proud.) I got in my understated SUV and drove past the woman whose mouth had not yet resumed the shut position.

I interviewed Kimberly who took her chances five years ago and broke into the remaining building through an open window via the boost-lift of her friend. (Warning: Please do not attempt this. This is private property and the place is watched carefully by the aforementioned woman during the day and the police during the night hours.) Kimberly said three workers died in the process of tearing down the building and, therefore, the destruction was stopped.

Once inside, she saw an old dresser and remnants of skis and odds and ends. She then proceeded down a long hallway. Suddenly, she heard this loud bang and then a deep, booming scream. She said it was like nothing she had ever heard before in her life. It was simply terrifying. She ran back to her point of entry and jumped out the window. She told her friend: "That's it. I'm done. Let's get out of here."

Over the years Henryville House has built a list of purported ghosts. From the woman who threw herself onto a burning hay bale to commit suicide to the maid who hanged herself at the basement stairs. These and other spirits have taken permanent residence at the Henryville Inn.

CHAPTER 24

Paranormal Investigating Basics

Best practices for safely investigating and documenting the paranormal.

When the New Jersey Ghost Hunters Society was founded in 1998, it followed the protocols set forth by the International Ghost Hunters Society. In recent years, I have modified one protocol: removing the camera strap from one's camera. Initially this was to prevent a false positive vortex from appearing in the photos. By removing the strap, we removed the possibility of the strap dangling in front of the camera's lens. However, today the digital cameras have shrunk in size and increased in functionality and cost. Therefore, it is permissible to keep the strap on one's camera provided the strap is securely wrapped around one's wrist. This will prevent the camera from being dropped and the strap from interfering with the photographic results.

The remainder of our Protocols are as follows:

1. Never investigate outside in rain, snow, or humid/wet weather.

Moisture will form condensation on your camera's lens creating a picture of orbs—many orbs! You can still hunt for EVPs, but refrain from this as well if the rain is falling so hard that it is very loud and will clutter the recording with background noise.

When investigating outside in the cold weather, it is important to hold your breath while taking a photo. The steam that is created from your breath against the cold air will show up as an amazing ectoplasmic vapor—just like cigarette smoke does.

2. Don't do "Drive By" Shootings.

Pulling up in your car at the local cemetery and hanging out the window to do a grab shot will result in dust orbs, possibly pollen orbs too given the time of year. Once your car comes to a halt, the dust from the road will trail up from behind and as you snap that picture, you'll get the multi-orb effect. Bear in mind that dust orbs and pollen orbs travel "in herds." They will usually appear as a swirling mass of orbs.

3. No smoking, eating, or drinking during an investigation.

The smoke will appear as ectoplasmic mist or vapor in your photos. The sounds of drinking and eating in the background will corrupt your audio recordings for EVP.

4. Professionalism and Reverence.

Always show reverence and respect for the deceased while investigating a cemetery. Additionally, show respect for the cemetery itself, again by not eating, drinking, or smoking and littering.

Pay close attention to the "No trespassing" signs if posted at the entrance of a cemetery. You must secure permission prior to investigating from the caretaker or parish head if it is a church cemetery. Sometimes you can register with the local police department to gain permission to be in the cemetery after dusk. I prefer to have written permission from the cemetery owner/caretaker, and still check in with the local police force. It's possible that frantic calls may be placed to the police from neighbors who live near the cemetery and are concerned seeing flashes (from the cameras) and people milling around.

5. Safety First!

Never investigate alone. Always be in teams of at least two people. Have your cell phone with you, but turn it off during the investigation. You can use two-way radios, but, again, you run the risk of having one go off just as an EVP is being recorded.

If you're doing a cemetery hunt and have acquired the necessary permission, it's best to get a lay of the land. Go there in the daylight to scope the place out. Take note of any fallen headstones or gopher holes, etc. Make sure you know where the exits are in case you do need to leave abruptly.

Take into consideration the area the cemetery is in as well. If the area has a reputation for being infested with drunken or drugged individuals or groups and societal misfits, don't go there to investigate. The living are more dangerous than the dead.

Investigation Prep

Always use new discs for the camcorder and clean memory cards for the digital camera. Lithium batteries should be fully charged and regular batteries replaced with new ones. Don't forget to pack extra batteries for your equipment. It only takes one greedy ghost to zap your equipment's battery power. Test and calibrate all equipment before leaving for the investigation. Remember to pack a pen, notepad, and your ID (ghost hunter business cards and driver's license).

Dress for Paranormal Success

Make sure you dress comfortably and weather appropriate. Wear sneakers for better footing. Pockets are a must. I have found that a fisherman vest works best. It's lightweight and can go over a bulky sweatshirt or jacket. It provides tons of pockets to store batteries, discs, audio recorders, cameras, etc. There's even a clip to attach the thermal scanner and/or flashlight. Speaking of light, there are woolen hats that have LED lights built in or you can buy a "head light" that secures by a strap to your head. I prefer the head strap one by Energizer® as it is LED powered and is capable of switching from white light to red light, which is beneficial when filming in infrared mode.

Remember to tie back long hair so a false positive vortex is not photographed. It only takes one strand of human hair to fall in front of the camera's lens to create this false positive.

On the Investigation—Making a Great Team

It's always best to keep your team to about five people for private in-home investigations. You don't want to show up at someone's house with a huge entourage and overwhelm them since they're probably on overload as it is with the activity they're experiencing.

Appoint a team leader. The team leader is the one who will be in contact with the homeowner or businessowner, coordinate the team members and their responsibilities, and collect the data from each member into a comprehensive Report of Findings.

Digital Audio (EVPs)
Digital Video (DVR and static camcorder)
Digital Still Camera
35 mm Camera
Thermal Scanner
EMF (Electromagnetic Field Strength Meter) or Mel Meter
Historical Researcher (usually this member is not on site for the investigation, but is at the library or town hall reviewing microfiche and various legal documents to piece together the history of the property being investigated)

Each team member can employ all their "gadgets" on the investigation. However, they are responsible for their review and submission of their assigned duty to the team leader for the Report of Findings.

Private Investigations

Before you arrive at the home, advise the contact person there to have prepared a "Chronology of Events." This report will help set the timeline from when they first noticed something "not quite right" up until the investigation.

138

Basic Agenda of an Investigation

Paperwork

Complete all permission and liability forms that your organization provides. If your team does not have these forms in place, make it a point to develop them. It is best to have permission from the homeowner or businessowner who is requesting the investigation in writing. Liability forms hold harmless the homeowner or businessowner in case someone on the investigative team is hurt or their equipment is damaged. Further, it covers your team should they accidentally damage something belonging to the homeowner or businessowner.

Next, complete a basic questionnaire to establish a baseline for each individual living in the household. This questionnaire should require demographics of each person living in the home or who is present for the investigation because they have had a paranormal experience when visiting. It should also ask if the person wears eyeglasses or contact lenses, hearing aids, and if they take prescribed medications. The medications can be a sensitive area to venture into, but some medications do have side effects of hallucinations and that could be the haunt the person is experiencing. It's important to be a professional when completing this questionnaire to assure the client that this information remains private and will not be shared or posted anywhere.

Interview

Review the homeowner's Chronology of Events. Make sure someone on the team is taking notes and that someone is recording the entire process of paperwork and interview. EVPs have been collected during these segments of the investigation.

Walk-through

Have the homeowner/businessowner give your team a tour of the place and point out the active spots as determined by the Chronology of Events log. This provides the team leader time and information to make the designations for equipment and team members' positions and duties.

Pack and Go

Don't overstay your welcome. If the investigation is capturing an abundance of evidence, then it is permissible to stay a little longer to complete the investigation. Otherwise, it is best to keep the investigation to no more than one hour and a half.

Report of Findings

Team members should complete their data review and send their findings to the team leader within a week of the investigation.

The historical researcher should compile historical information on the land, the building or house itself, the town's history, and any local tragedies or disasters, such as airplane crashes, train derailments, floods, or fires. Most historical researchers spend the bulk of their time at the library reviewing microfiche or at the town hall reviewing deed transfers and birth and death certificates. Fortunately, more and more of this information is being scanned and uploaded to various genealogy websites.

The team leader should coordinate all the members' reports and evidence into a concise Report of Findings to be presented to the homeowner in person or emailed to the homeowner within two weeks from the date of the investigation. Conclusions should be clearly defined at the end of the report. What the homeowner or business owner opts to do in light of the evidence presented is completely up to him or her.

CHAPTER 25

Photographic Anomalies

How do ghosts appear in pictures?

e Pocono

Author saw this orb in her peripheral vision and managed to capture it in a digital photo.

Orbs

A lot has changed and advanced since I first started ghost hunting in 1993. Over the years, ghost hunters have come to dismiss orbs completely. That's not a fair treatment of the little ball of light. I agree that probably ninety-nine percent of them are airborne particulates, such as dust, pollen, pet dander, and insects. However, there is that one percent of the time when the orb is genuine spirit energy. This can be confirmed as such with concurrent evidence captured at the time of the orb photograph such as an EVP, temperature drop, or EMF spike.

Sometimes the orb is visible to the human eye. I had this experience while staying at Oheka Castle on Long Island, New York. I saw this ball of light fly by me in my peripheral vision, and I managed to get my camera and take a picture in the direction I saw it flying. It worked. There was this single orb above the four-poster bed. Another time, I was on a private investigation, and while taking photos in the basement using a 35 mm camera, I saw an orb in the light of the flash. I dismissed it as my imagination, but when I got the film developed from that investigation, that was the only picture that had an orb in it.

Vortex (vortices, plural)

A vortex is a white tornado-like presentation in photos. Some theorize that this is a cluster of orbs or spirits getting ready to separate. Others theorize the vortex represents a portal being opened through which spirits may pass from their world to ours and back again. The best example I have is one that was

Vortex appears next to the author in her living room in October 1997. Photo was taken with a 35 mm camera.

captured on 35 mm film in my then-living room in 1997. Friday, October 17, 1997, my then-husband and I took a tour of Fairview Cemetery in Westfield with a friend of ours who was also a Westfield police officer. It was interesting to see the List family graves and the grave that was broken into in 1982. (This is the same cemetery that singer Whitney Houston is laid to rest.) We took many pictures that night.

The next night, Saturday, October 18, I was to perform at a Bat Mitzvah as "L'Aura Aura" giving Tarot card readings. The employer requested I have pictures taken of me in the costume so she could use those to secure more psychic entertaining work for me. My then-husband took two pictures of me using the same camera that we used the night before in the cemetery.

Sunday, October 19, I got up early to make my mother her birthday cake. I could not find the paddle attachment for my standing mixer. I looked in all the usual places: cabinet, dish drainer, and dish washer. Then I began to look in the not-so-usual places: the living room, bookcases, and under the beds in each bedroom. It was gone. I had to call my Mom and tell her the sad news that I would not be able to make her birthday cake. She said: "That's okay. Just bring my grandsons up so I can see them."

As we loaded up the minivan with kids and all their paraphernalia, I remembered I had my older son's school pictures. Knowing all the relatives would be at my parents' house, I decided to take all but the 8 x 10 with me to distribute thereby saving on postage. I placed the 8 x 10 on top of my jewelry box on my dresser and took the remaining photos in the envelope.

After we returned home, I went to the bedroom to get the 8 x 10 so I could frame it. It was gone. Now I knew something was wrong. This wasn't my typical memory failure or ability to misplace things in a single bound. I resolved that once the boys went to sleep, I would smudge the entire house.

The next day, Monday, I picked up the developed photos from the weekend. There was a vortex present in the lower right corner of the picture of a gravestone from the Friday night investigation. I was so happy; it was my very first vortex. Then I got to the photos taken of me on Saturday night, and I saw the vortex next to me. I was right. It had followed me home from the cemetery. I got up to to get a glass of water, and my favorite glass was in the sink with other dirty dishes. I opted to treat myself and take one of our "good glasses," the ones used for when we had visitors above three feet in height; and there was my son's 8 x 10 lying on top of those glasses.

Not only did I capture my first vortex, but I learned my first valuable lesson about smudging. It is part of the NJGHS protocols to smudge oneself after each cemetery hunt or private, in-home investigation. Trust me; you don't want to bring "your work" home with you.

Ectoplasmic Mist or Vapor as photographed using a 35 mm camera.

Ectoplasmic Mist or Vapor

This is an amorphous cloudy presentation. I have found it to be the pre-cursor to a full-body apparition. For example, while ghost hunting on Sach's Covered Bridge in Gettysburg in 1998, I captured an ectoplasmic vapor while taking a picture of the ceiling of the bridge. I was using 35 mm and, therefore, did not know at that time I'd captured anything. Since it was so cold out, I wanted to return to the warm hotel. We left. The next morning while convening for the final day of the ghost conference, a group of people were ecstatic over witnessing of a full-body apparition of a cavalry unit that came charging across Sach's Covered Bridge and disappeared into the adjoining field. This happened ten minutes after we left.

Full-Body Apparition

This is the "holy grail" for ghost hunters, and it is very rare to actually capture one in a photo. It is theorized that ghosts are at a very high vibratory frequency, and that renders them invisible to the human eye. Our cameras function at a compatible frequency and, therefore, are able to photograph the spirits. Typically, a full-body apparition will appear as a gauzy or dusty outline of a human form, but sometimes the ghost is adept at slowing down its vibratory rate and manifesting more solidly. Sometimes, they do this so well, that they are visible to the naked eye. The best, and most famous, example of a full-body apparition is the Brown Lady of Raynham Hall. This was captured in 1936 during a photo shoot for *Country Life* magazine in England.

CHAPTER 26

EVPs—Classifying Ghostly Recordings

e Pocono

Electromagnetic Voice Phenomena (EVP) is a recording of spirit voices. Originally, these recordings were captured on analog reel-to-reel or cassette tape, but today digital is primarily employed. The advantage of the digital recorder is that it does not have the cranking sounds of the tape advancing and, therefore, can capture the slightest whisper with ease and clarity. Further, the digital audio file can be transferred to a computer where certain audio software can be used to clean up the recording by removing background noise and amplifying the foreground sound. Some software translates the voice recordings to visual documentation on the computer screen so that the "voice path" can be analyzed.

It's best to start each investigation with every team member stating their name on the recorders being used so that the sound of their voice and its path can be used to compare and contrast against possible EVPs captured during the investigation later on during data review.

Today the standard for classifying EVPs is as follows:

Class A

Perfectly clear and discernable voice and words with the possibility of being heard "real time" by the investigator

Class B

Not heard during the investigation but is heard upon playback of the recording. It requires several playbacks to determine what exactly is being communicated.

Class C

Common EVP of whispers, grunts, groans, and indecipherable verbiage captured, again not audible to the human ear.

Class D

So poor a recording that it is usually dismissed as simply background noise.

Directory of Paranormal Organizations, Researchers, and Tours

C.O.R.E. Phenomena Research
John Hotchkiss, Co-Founder
Saylorsburg, Pennsylvania
corephenomena@gmail.com

Columns Museum—home of Milford Historical Society
608 Broad Street
Milford, Pennsylvania 18337
570-296-8126
http://pikehistorical.org/

Covered Bridge Inn
4300 Little Gap Road
Palmerton, Pennsylvania 18071
610-826-5400
http://coveredbridgeinn.net/

Dickson City Paranormal Investigators
Anthony Arcuri, Director
Dickson City, Pennsylvania
570-780-8858
thrdbase89@aol.com

Dusk Till Dawn Paranormal Investigations
Eric Pensyl, Founder
Central and Southern New Jersey, Philadelphia (greater
Philadelphia) and Allentown, PA
www.dusktilldawnparanormalinvestigators.com

East Stroudsburg University
200 Prospect Street
East Stroudsburg, Pennsylvania 18301
570-422-3211
www.esu.edu/

Flagstaff
Jim Thorpe, Pennsylvania 18229
www.flagstaffresort.net/index.html

Ghost Tours of Jim Thorpe
www.jimthorperotary.org/ghostwalks.cfm
Tour Guide: Carleen Ladden, cladden@ptd.net

Haunted Milford Walking Tour
Tim Kelly
570-832-0385
https://m.facebook.com/HauntedMilford/

Hotel Fauchère
401 Broad Street
Milford, Pennsylvania 18337
570-409-1212
www.hotelfauchere.com/welcome/welcome.php

Inn at Jim Thorpe
24 Broadway
Jim Thorpe, Pennsylvania 18229
800-329-2599
www.innjt.com/

Jorgenson's at the Dimmick Inn
101 E. Hartford Street
Milford, Pennsylvania 18337
570-296-4021
www.jorgensonsdimmickinn.com/

Lake House—Hotel of Horror haunted house
Corner of Wilkes-Barre Turnpike and Cherry Valley Road
Saylorsburg, Pennsylvania 18353
570-992-3278
www.hotelofhorror.com/

Linda Zimmermann, author/lecturer
www.gotozim.com/
www.amazon.com/s/ref=dp_byline_sr_book_1?ie=UTF8&tex
t=Linda+Zimmermann&search-alias=books&field-author=L
inda+Zimmermann&sort=relevancerank

Markou Paranormal
Ted & Kim Markou, investigators
(570) 982-8613
Email: kimmarkou@gmail.com
Facebook: www.facebook.com/Markou-
Paranormal-240513672711857

Mauch Chunk Opera House
14 West Broadway
Jim Thorpe, Pennsylvania 18229
570-325-0249
http://mcohjt.com/

Memorytown
432 Grange Road
Mount Pocono, Pennsylvania 18344
570-839-1680
www.memorytownusa.com/

New Jersey Ghost Hunters Society
(Stay tuned to the Presentations page of this website for my appearances and presentations)
http://njghs.net

NEPA Paranormal—Bob Christopher
Wilkes-Barre, Pennsylvania 18702
570-328-4723
www.NEPAparanormal.com

Old Jail Museum
128 West Broadway
Jim Thorpe, Pennsylvania 18229
570-325-5259
www.theoldjailmuseum.com/

Pocono Cinema & Cultural Center
88 South Courtland Street
East Stroudsburg, Pennsylvania 18301
570-421-3456
http://poconocommunitytheater.org/

Pocono Indian Museum
5425 Milford Road/RT 209
East Stroudsburg, Pennsylvania 18302
570-588-9338
www.poconoindianmuseumonline.com/shop/

Sorrenti's Cherry Valley Winery
130 Lower Cherry Valley Road
Saylorsburg, Pennsylvania 18353
570-992-2255
www.cherryvalleyvineyards.com/

St. Mark's Church
21 Race Street
Jim Thorpe, Pennsylvania 18229
570-325-2241
http://stmarkandjohn.org/

Sullivan Paranormal
Barb O'Rourke
Monticello, New York
http://sullivanparanormal.wix.com/sullivanparanormalsociety

Tannersville Inn
RT 611 (use Exit 299 off RT 80)
Tannersville, Pennsylvania 18372
570-629-3131
www.tannersvilleinn.com/

The Inn at Pocono Manor
RT 314, One Manor Drive
Pocono Manor, Pennsylvania 18349
570-839-7111
www.poconomanor.com/

The Shawnee Inn and Golf Resort
100 Shawnee Inn Drive
Shawnee on the Delaware, Pennsylvania 18356
570-424-4000
www.shawneeinn.com/

Tom X Pub
100 Tom X Road
East Stroudsburg, Pennsylvania 18302
570-223-5025
www.tomxpub.com/

Bibliography

Adams III, Charles J. *Coal Country Ghosts, Legends and Lore: Schuylkill and Carbon Counties Pennsylvania.* Reading, PA: Exeter House Books, 2007.

Adams III, Charles J. *Pocono Ghosts, Legends and Lore.* Reading, PA: Exeter House Books, 1991.

Adams III, Charles J. *Pocono Ghosts, Legends and Lore Book Two.* Reading, PA: Exeter House Books, 1995.

Biddle, Kenneth. *Haunted Lehigh Valley.* Atglen, PA: Schiffer Publishing Ltd., 2010.

Boyer, Dennis. *Once Upon a Hex.* Rochester, MN: Lisa Loucks Christenson Publishing, LLC., 2004.

Guiley, Rosemary Ellen. *Ghosthunting Pennsylvania.* Cincinnati, OH: Clerisy Press, 2009.

Hauck, Dennis William. *Haunted Places The National Directory: Ghostly Abodes, Sacred Sites, UFO Landings, and Other Supernatural Locations.* New York: Penguin Group Inc., 1994, 1996, 2002.

Lake, Matt. *Weird Pennsylvania—Your Travel Guide to Pennsylvania's Local Legends and Best Kept Secrets.* New York: Sterling Publishing Co., Inc., 2005.

Mack, Carol and Dinah. *A Field Guide to Demons, Fairies, Fallen Angels, & Other Subversive Spirits.* New York Arcade Publishing, Inc., 1998.

McBride, Betty Lou, and Kathleen McBride Sisack. *Ghosts of the Molly Maguires? A Decade of Strange & Unusual Happenings in the Old Jail Jim Thorpe, Pennsylvania.* Bethlehem, Pennsylvania: Christmas City Printing Co., 2006.

McBride, Thomas, and Betty Lou. *A Molly Maguire Tragedy: Hand of Innocence, True Story of the Molly Maguires and Thomas P. Fisher.* Bethlehem, Pennsylvania: Christmas City Printing Co., 2013.

Website Resources

Introduction
www.accessible-archives.com

Chapter 1
www.tannersvilleinn.com

Chapter 2
http://mcohjt.com

Chapter 3
www.cherryvalleyvineyards.com
www.nanticoke-lenape.info
https://archive.org
https://books.google.com

Chapter 4
www.poconorecord.com
http://articles.mcall.com
http://articles.mcall.com
www.poconorecord.com
www.buckhillinn.com
www.wuhwild.com
http://sometimes-interesting.com
www.buckhillfalls.org/history.html

Chapter 6
www.poconorecord.com
www.innjt.com
http://mlgallagher.com

Chapter 7
www.theoldjailmuseum.com
http://mlgallagher.com

Chapter 8

http://wnep.com
http://beforeitsnews.com
http://unsolved.com
http://wnep.com
www.historicmysteries.com

Chapter 9
www.shawneeinn.com
www.nepaparanormal.com

Chapter 10
www.tomxpub.com
www.tomxpub.com

Chapter 11
http://hotelfauchere.com
http://hotelfauchere.com
www.hotelfauchere.com
https://books.google.com

Chapter 12
www.tobyhannatwphistory.org

Chapter 13
www.hauntinglypa.com
http://hauntsandhistory.blogspot.com
http://pikehistorical.org/

Chapter 14
www.lehighvalleylive.com

Chapter 15
www.poconoghosts.com
www.poconorecord.com
www.monroehistorical.org
http://latenighthorrorhotel.blogspot.com
www.poconorecord.com
www.poconorecord.com
www.monroehistorical.org
https://www.youtube.com

Chapter 16
www.wfmz.com/
www.asapackermansion.com
http://stmarkandjohn.org
www.bhchorale.org/

Chapter 18
www.jorgensonsdimmickinn.com
https://youtu.be

Chapter 19
www.livingplaces.com
http://lancasterpa.com

Chapter 20
www.findagrave.com
www.poconohistory.com
http://thestroudcourier.com
http://hauntsandhistory.blogspot.com/
https://sites.google.com
www.dusktilldawnparanormalinvestigators.com
www.dusktilldawnparanormalinvestigators.com
www.poconorecord.com

Chapter 22
www.monroehistorical.org/
http://poconocommunitytheater.org/
http://archives.timesleader.com

Chapter 23
http://standardspeaker.com
www.flagstaffresort.net/history.html
www.tnonline.com
http://carboncountymagazine.com
www.parksidechapelofhenryville.org
www.monroehistorical.org

About the Author

Growing up in New Jersey, **L'Aura Hladik Hoffman** heard the story of her great-grandmother's ownership of one the wallets made from the human skin of Antoine LeBlanc. Her mother was the bookkeeper for the Wedgewood Inn, which was originally the Sayre Farm—the very site where Antoine committed the murders of Mr. & Mrs. Sayre and their servant girl, Phoebe, in 1833. It is no surprise L'Aura went on to research ghosts and founded the NJ Ghost Hunters Society in 1998, which to date is New Jersey's largest paranormal investigating organization.

As a paranormal investigator, L'Aura has stayed at the famously haunted Myrtles Plantation in St. Francisville, Louisiana. Other ghost hunting explorations have taken her to Chicago, Savannah, San Diego, and New Orleans. Internationally, she's investigated several Irish haunted castles, most notably Leap Castle (County Offaly, Ireland).

L'Aura has appeared on the nationally syndicated television show *Montel Williams* (UPN Network), and *The Morning Show with Mike & Juliet* (Fox Network) to discuss her ghostly findings. Internationally, she's appeared on various news shows and documentaries airing on Telemundo (Latin America), M6 (France), and Maximus Films (Germany).

Other books by L'Aura include *Ghosthunting New Jersey* (2008) and *Ghosthunting New York City* (2010).

When not investigating or writing about the paranormal, L'Aura enjoys life on the mountain in Pennsylvania. Between baking award-winning cupcakes and developing a sustainable farm with her husband, Kent, she still finds time to care for their two dogs, six cats, seven chickens, and two grown sons, Brian and Trent.

e Pocono

More Creepy Choices
from Schiffer

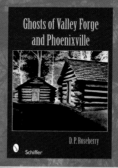